THE CREATIVE
Pasta
COOKBOOK

COURAGE BOOKS
AN IMPRINT OF RUNNING PRESS
PHILADELPHIA · LONDON

Watercolor illustrations by Sally Damant

Designed by Stonecastle Graphics

Edited by Jillian Stewart

U.S. adaptation: Josephine Bacon, Chanterelle Ltd

4950
© 1997 CLB International

Printed in Singapore

9 8 7 6 5 4 3 2 1
Digit on the right indicates the number of this printing
Library of Congress Cataloging-in-Publication Number 96-71946
ISBN 0-7624-0097-8

This book was produced by CLB International, Godalming, Surrey, U.K.

Published by Courage Books, an imprint of
Running Press Book Publishers
125 South Twenty-second Street
Philadelphia, Pennsylvania 19103-4399

13.95

Contents

Introduction
page 8

Introduction

Pasta is as old as the hills. There are several legends as to how it came to be invented, such as the story about the Chinese girl who got talking to her sailor boyfriend and let the dumpling dough boil over the pot until it formed into strings hanging over the sides. This is not very credible, in fact the person who first told the story obviously didn't know how to make pasta! Nor is the tale of how Marco Polo first brought pasta to Italy from China. The Greeks and Romans ate pasta a thousand years before Marco Polo, that intrepid traveler, voyaged to Cathay in the early 14th century.

Pasta was particularly popular in the Ancient World because it is easy to make and quick to cook, as well as being very filling in the days when potatoes were unknown outside Peru. In fact, it is the fast food of both the ancient and the modern world. We associate pasta-eating mainly with the Italians and the Chinese, but pasta is popular throughout Asia and southern Europe, and it can be found in a wide variety of forms. Most pasta is made from wheat, but the Chinese also use rice noodles (angel hair pasta or cellophane noodles, that are soaked in water to swell and soften before cooking) and the Japanese are fond of *soba*, buckwheat noodles.

Time was, dieticians advised slimmers against eating pasta as it was reputed to be fattening. Now we know different. Pasta – ground grains mixed with water and dried, then later boiled – is a complex carbohydrate. This means that the body has to use up calories digesting it, making it a slimming food. If there is anything fattening about pasta, it is the delicious but potentially fattening sauces that go with it. However, these sauces need not be fattening and this book has plenty of suggestions for slimming them down, using yogurt instead of heavy cream, for instance.

Pasta is probably the most versatile of foodstuffs. It can be eaten at any meal (the Hungarians like boiled noodles sprinkled with ground nuts or poppyseeds and sugar for breakfast!) and for any course. Small pasta is the perfect addition to soups to make them nourishing and filling, and a small portion tossed with sauce and vegetables makes a great appetizer. As an entrée, pasta can be coated with a sauce containing meats and vegetables, and is an appropriate side dish for almost any entrée imaginable. Pasta is even eaten as a dessert, especially in cold countries where it makes a comforting winter sweet dish. Best of all, pasta is the great standby for unexpected company. It keeps almost indefinitely in the store cabinet, especially if it is inside an airtight container. A package of pasta, a can of tomatoes, a few herbs and spices, and whatever you can find in the refrigerator – and you can feed all your neighbors at once if they happen to drop by!

The pasta quantities in this book have all been given by weight. Pasta is hard to measure in cups, since the measurement depends on pasta size, whether the pasta is fresh or dried, and so on. It is easy to work out the weight you will need, simply by looking at the weight on the package label and dividing or multiplying it as necessary. Weights do not need to be totally accurate, since they represent a proportion of the liquid needed to swell the pasta and cook it. You can always adjust the liquid used for cooking it if you find you have under- or overestimated.

This book covers every kind of pasta recipe, from soup to desserts. There are old favorites, such as Minestroni and Minestra from Italy, and unusual soups such as the spicy Chicken and Vegetable Soup with Curry from Thailand. There are seafood recipes such as Shell Pasta with Taramasalata, a fish roe appetizer from Greece, Turkey, and Cyprus, and the classic Linguini with Clams. Combining pasta with meats is easy if you follow the recipes using standard meats such as chicken and turkey and strongly flavored variety meats, such as liver and sweetbreads, which combine especially well with the mild flavor of pasta. There are boiled pastas and plenty of baked pastas, such as Pastitsio, a great favorite in the eastern Mediterranean.

Hot or cold, winter or summer, pasta is the most versatile of dishes. And it is becoming even more so. Every day, the grocery stores and supermarkets offer new varieties, in interesting shapes, colors, and flavors. The recipes in this book do not specify a type of pasta too closely, so that you can experiment with whatever kinds you like. Only the size and approximate shape (soup pasta, small pasta, penne, etc) are suggested. Be adventurous, try new and amusing varieties (you can now get pasta in American flag shapes!) and flavored pasta, such as black linguini flavored with cuttlefish ink, and tomato-flavored red or spinach-flavored green fettuccini. Herb-flavored pastas are becoming more and more popular. You could serve a different pasta shape and flavor for every meal every day of the week for months and still have more to choose from! So bring the variety of pasta to your table with choice recipes from this exciting cookbook!

Soups

Pasta turns a cup of broth into a real soup! This is no secret; it has been known to the Italians, Chinese and East Europeans for centuries. Whether you use tiny pasta shapes – spirals, stars, rice-shaped pasta grains, or alphabet pasta – vermicelli, or even ravioli, a soup becomes both filling and more interesting with the addition of pasta. We offer a variety of soups, traditional and modern, popular and exotic, from the ever-popular Minestrone and Minestra to exotic Thai soups, Chicken Broth with Herbed Ravioli, perfect for company, and an unusual tomato soup with a hint of horseradish. There is something to please everyone, including vegetarians, finicky eaters, and even kids who seem to have taken an illogical dislike to soup! Give them a big bowl of chickpea or bean soup, laced with generous portions of tiny pasta in cute shapes, and they will become so interested in what they are eating, they will forget to complain.

Here again, pasta comes to the rescue when you have to find something quick and filling for unexpected company. A can of consommé, jazzed up with pasta, will produce a soup fit for a prince!

In addition to small soup shapes, the thin strands of vermicelli and capelli d'angeli (angel hair pasta) are very suitable for soups, as are the Chinese cellophane noodles.

Do not let wheat pasta cook too long in soup or it will become soggy. Add small shapes and home-made ravioli five minutes before removing the soup from the heat, larger shapes and dry ravioli should cook for 7 or 8 minutes. Whole-wheat pasta may take a minute or two longer to cook. Cellophane noodles, on the other hand, should not be cooked at all. Ladle a cup or so of soup from the pot into a bowl and let the cellophane noodles soak in it for 10 minutes. As soon as you are ready to serve the soup, pour the noodles and soup back into the pot. Happy eating!

Minestrone

There are many recipes for this classic Italian soup. This one has a rich, pesto-like mayonnaise added as a delicious garnish.

SERVES 4-6

½ cup navy or Great Northern beans, soaked overnight

2 Tbsps olive oil

4-ounce piece bacon or salt pork

1 carrot, diced

2 medium potatoes, diced

¼ cup peas (shelled, fresh or frozen)

½ zucchini, diced

½ cup pasta shells

Sauce

10 fresh basil leaves

1 Tbsp pine nuts

1 egg yolk

1 clove garlic, finely chopped

½ cup olive oil

Salt and freshly ground black pepper

⅓ cup finely grated Cheddar or Parmesan

Rinse and drain the beans. Heat the olive oil in a large saucepan and gently sauté the beans and bacon for 1 minute. Add plenty of water and cook for about 45 minutes until the beans are tender.

To make the sauce, crush together the basil and pine nuts in a pestle and mortar. Blend in the egg yolk and garlic, then gradually whisk in the oil until the sauce thickens like mayonnaise. Alternatively, briefly process the basil, nuts, egg, and garlic in a blender and pour in the oil in a thin stream with the machine running. Season with salt and pepper. Add the grated cheese to the sauce, stir well, and set aside.

Add the carrot, potatoes, and peas to the beans, cook for 15 minutes, then add the zucchini and pasta and cook for a final 15 minutes. Remove the bacon and serve the soup accompanied by the sauce.

Time: Preparation takes 10 minutes, plus overnight soaking. Cooking takes 1 hour 15 minutes.

Variation: Substitute canned navy or Great Northern beans to save the lengthy soaking and cooking time.

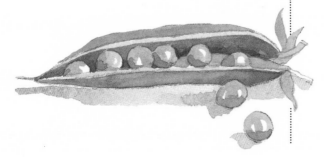

Chicken Soup with — Vermicelli —

This light, nutritious soup is the perfect appetizer for a Mediterranean-style meal.

SERVES 4

3 Tbsps butter

1 carrot, finely sliced

1 bayleaf

1 onion, finely sliced

1 (about 2¼ pounds) chicken carcass (bones and meat)

½ leek (white part only), finely sliced

Salt and freshly ground black pepper

2 ounces vermicelli

2 Tbsps chopped fresh chives

Heat the butter in a large saucepan and gently fry the carrot and bayleaf for 2 minutes. Add the onion and continue cooking for 2 minutes.

Add the chicken carcass, roughly chopped, and fry, shaking the pan, for a few minutes. Add enough water to cover, stir in the leek, and season with salt and pepper. Cook over a moderate heat for 45 minutes, adding extra water as necessary.

Strain the contents of the pan through a fine strainer, reserving the broth only. Pour the broth into a clean saucepan, bring to a boil, and add the vermicelli. Cook for about 2 minutes, then serve, sprinkled with the chopped chives.

Time: Preparation takes 10 minutes, cooking takes about 1 hour.

Beef & Noodle — Soup —

This is a rich, filling soup, deliciously flavored with marinated beef.

SERVES 4

8 ounces beef tenderloin

1 clove garlic, chopped

1 green onion (scallion), chopped

2 Tbsps soy sauce

Salt and freshly ground black pepper

8 ounces fresh noodles or fine fettuccini

Few drops of sesame oil

3 cups beef broth

Few drops of chili sauce

1 Tbsp chopped fresh chives

Cut the beef into thin slices. Sprinkle the chopped garlic, green onion (scallion), and soy sauce over the meat, and season with salt and pepper. Leave to marinate for 15 minutes.

Cook the noodles in boiling, salted water to which a few drops of sesame oil have been added, until tender. Rinse the noodles and set aside to drain.

Bring the broth to a boil and add the beef and its marinade. Simmer gently for 10 minutes. Stir in the noodles, season with a few drops of chili sauce, and simmer for just long enough to heat the noodles through. Serve garnished with the chives.

Time: Preparation takes 10 minutes, plus marinating. Cooking takes 20 minutes.

Tomato Soup

This unusual tomato soup contains horseradish. Use two tablespoons of horseradish sauce if fresh horseradish is not available.

SERVES 4-6

2 Tbsps butter or margarine
1 small onion, chopped
1 small green bell pepper, chopped
1 Tbsp all-purpose flour
1 quart beef broth
1 pound tomatoes, chopped
2 Tbsps tomato paste
Salt and freshly ground black pepper
4 ounces macaroni
1 Tbsp grated horseradish
2 Tbsps sour cream
1 Tbsp chopped fresh parsley

Heat the butter in a pan, add the onion and green bell pepper, then cover and cook for 5 minutes. Add the flour and stir. Cook for 1 minute then add the broth, tomatoes, and tomato paste. Bring to a boil, stirring continuously, then simmer for 15 minutes.

Blend the soup until smooth in a blender or food processor, then strain it through a sieve. Return it to the pan and season with salt and pepper. Add the macaroni 10-15 minutes before serving and stir occasionally. Stir in the grated horseradish and garnish with the sour cream and parsley. Serve immediately.

Time: Preparation takes 15 minutes, cooking takes 40 minutes.

Variation: Use some other pasta shape, but ensure it is thoroughly cooked before serving the soup.

Minestra

This is a substantial variation on the classic Minestrone.

SERVES 4-6

1 onion
1 carrot
1 stick celery
2 Tbsps olive oil
3¾ pints water
Salt and freshly ground black pepper
2 cups fresh spinach
2 tomatoes
4 ounces macaroni
2 cloves garlic, finely chopped
2 Tbsps chopped fresh parsley
1 tsp chopped fresh rosemary
4 Tbsps grated Parmesan cheese

Cut the onion, carrot, and celery into thick matchstick strips. Heat the oil in a large, heavy pan and fry the vegetable strips until just browning, stirring occasionally. Add the water, salt, and pepper and simmer for 20 minutes.

Meanwhile, wash the spinach leaves and shred them. Add to the soup and cook for 10 minutes. Skin the tomatoes and chop them roughly, removing the seeds. Add the tomatoes, macaroni, garlic, parsley, and rosemary to the soup, and simmer a further 10 minutes. Adjust the seasoning. Serve with grated Parmesan cheese.

Time: Preparation takes 15 minutes, cooking takes 45 minutes.

Cook's Tip: Use freshly grated Parmesan, as the pre-packaged variety will spoil the flavor of this delicate soup.

Spiced Fried Soup

This Classic Indonesian soup is so substantial that it can be served as a complete meal in itself.

SERVES 4

4-8 Tbsps oil

1 clove garlic

1 pound (2 cups) chicken breast meat, skinned and cut into small pieces

1 cup tofu, drained and cut into 1-inch cubes

2 Tbsps raw cashew nuts

4 shallots, roughly chopped

1 carrot, very thinly sliced

⅔ cup snow peas

2 ounces Chinese egg noodles, soaked for 5 minutes in hot water and drained thoroughly

3¼ pints chicken broth

Juice of 1 lime

¼ tsp ground turmeric

2 curry leaves

1 tsp grated fresh root ginger

1 Tbsp soy sauce

Salt and freshly ground black pepper

Heat 2-3 Tbsps of the oil in a wok or large skillet. Add the garlic clove and cook until brown. Remove the garlic from the pan and discard it. Add the chicken pieces and cook in the oil until they begin to brown. Remove the meat using a slotted spoon and drain well on paper towels.

Add a little more oil and cook the tofu until lightly browned. Remove and drain well. Add the raw cashew nuts and cook, stirring constantly, until toasted. Remove and drain well. Add a little more oil and fry the shallots and carrot until lightly browned. Stir in the snow peas and cook for 1 minute. Remove from the pan and drain well.

Reheat the oil in the wok until it is very hot, adding any remaining from the original amount. Add the drained noodles and cook quickly until brown on one side. Turn over and brown the other side. Reduce the heat and add the broth. Stir in the lime juice, turmeric, curry leaves, ginger, soy sauce, and seasoning.

Cover and simmer gently for 10 minutes, stirring occasionally to prevent the noodles from sticking to the pan. Add the fried ingredients, season to taste, and heat through for 5 minutes. Serve immediately.

Time: Preparation takes 15 minutes, cooking takes about 50 minutes.

Ravioli Soup

The secret of success in this recipe is to use a good home-made broth.

SERVES 4

1 cup pasta dough (see page 18)
3 slices Parma ham or prosciutto, cut into very thin strips
2 Tbsps butter
1 egg, beaten
1 quart chicken broth
Nutmeg
Salt and freshly ground black pepper
2 Tbsps light cream
1 sprig tarragon, leaves stripped off and cut into thin strips

Prepare the pasta dough and roll it very thinly, either with a rolling pin or by passing it through a pasta machine. Cut it into rectangles. Place a little Parma ham and butter on one half of each piece, then brush the edges of the dough with the beaten egg. Fold each rectangle in half to form a square and pinch the edges well with your fingers to seal. Cut into neat squares or various shapes, using a ravioli cutter, and pinch the edges to seal if necessary.

Bring the broth to a boil in a large saucepan and season with nutmeg, salt, and pepper. Tip the ravioli into the broth and cook for about 2-5 minutes, depending on the thickness of the ravioli. They will float when cooked. Stir the cream into the soup just before serving and sprinkle with the strips of tarragon. Serve hot.
Time: Preparation takes about 40 minutes, cooking takes 10 minutes.
Cook's Tip: Cook the ravioli gently in the broth – it may burst open if it is cooked too vigorously.

Chickpea Soup

This is a substantial soup, suitable for cold winter days.

SERVES 4

1 cup dried chickpeas
3 Tbsps olive oil
2 cloves garlic
1½ cups canned plum tomatoes, chopped
3 cups chicken broth
1 Tbsp torn fresh basil leaves
Salt and freshly ground black pepper
1¼ cups small pasta shapes for soup
3 Tbsps grated Parmesan cheese

Cover the chickpeas with cold water and soak overnight. Discard the water and place the chickpeas in a large, heavy pan with enough water to cover. Bring to a boil, cover and simmer for 1 hour, or until tender. Check the water occasionally to ensure that the chickpeas do not boil dry.

Heat the olive oil in a heavy saucepan or Dutch oven, and sauté the whole garlic cloves until browned. Remove and discard the garlic. Add the tomatoes and their juice, the broth and torn basil, and cook for 20 minutes. Add the drained chickpeas and season to taste. Stir well and simmer for 10 minutes.

Return the soup to a boil and add the pasta, then cook, stirring frequently, for 10 minutes. Mix in half of the Parmesan cheese. Serve immediately, with the remaining Parmesan sprinkled on top.
Time: Preparation takes 5 minutes, plus overnight soaking. Cooking takes 1 hour 20 minutes.
Variation: Replace the dried chickpeas with canned chickpeas to save time.

Meatball Soup

A satisfying soup for a cold winter's day. The meatballs are cooked separately in the oven as they keep a better shape and texture than if they are boiled.

SERVES 4

1 pound beef bones

1 carrot, chopped

1 onion, chopped

1 stick celery, chopped

1 egg, beaten

8 ounces ground beef

4 tbps bread crumbs

Salt and freshly ground black pepper

1 Tbsp oil

14-ounce can plum tomatoes

6 ounces small pasta shapes for soup

1 Tbsp chopped fresh parsley

Place the beef bones, carrot, onion, and celery in a large saucepan, and cover with cold water. Bring to a boil, then cover and simmer for 1½ hours. Meanwhile, mix together the egg, ground beef, bread crumbs, and plenty of seasoning. Roll the mixture into small balls about the size of golf balls and place in a roasting pan with the oil. Bake in an oven preheated to 375 degrees for 40 minutes, turning occasionally.

Strain the broth into a saucepan. Press the tomatoes and their juice through a strainer and add to the broth. Bring to a boil and simmer for 15 minutes. Add the pasta shapes and cook for 10 minutes, stirring frequently. Add the meatballs, adjust the seasoning, and stir in the parsley. Serve hot.

Time: Preparation takes 10 minutes, cooking takes 1 hour 40 minutes.

Cook's Tip: If you cannot buy beef bones, cook the vegetables in a good beef broth for about 30 minutes.

Herb Ravioli with Chicken Broth

This recipe is a soup and pasta dish combined. Home-made ravioli dough is coated with fresh herbs and cooked in a chicken broth flavored with rosemary.

SERVES 4

1½ cups all-purpose flour
1 egg, beaten
1 small bunch fresh chervil
1 small bunch fresh flat-leaved parsley
1 quart chicken broth
1 tsp dried rosemary
Salt and freshly ground black pepper

Place the flour and a good pinch of salt in a large mixing bowl and make a well in the center. Add the beaten egg and knead the mixture into a ball, using first a fork and then your fingers. Add a little olive oil or water if the dough is too dry. Knead the dough until smooth, then cover and set it aside to rest for 30 minutes.

Pass the dough through a pasta machine, flouring both sides of the dough as it goes through the rollers to prevent it sticking. Cut the dough into long, wide strips with a knife. Alternatively, roll the dough out thinly with a rolling pin and cut into strips. Spread out half of the strips on your work surface. Remove the leaves from the chervil and parsley and spread out on the pasta strips. Place the remaining strips of dough on top, press down well all along the strips with your fingers, and then once again run the strips through the rollers of the pasta machine, or re-roll with a rolling pin until the pasta is very thin and you can see the herbs through it. Heat the broth and rosemary together in a large saucepan until it comes to a boil. Season with salt and pepper. Cut the dough into ravioli shapes, add to the boiling broth, and cook for 2-4 minutes, or until they float to the surface. Serve in shallow soup plates.

Time: Preparation takes about 1 hour, cooking takes about 15 minutes.

Thai Beef Soup

This delicious Thai recipe is an excellent soup to serve when company are coming.

SERVES 4

2 Tbsps oil

8 ounces sirloin steak, cut into thin strips

1 small onion, chopped

2 sticks celery, sliced diagonally

3¼ pints beef broth

1 Tbsp chopped fresh coriander (cilantro)

2 kaffir lime leaves

1-inch piece fresh root ginger, peeled and thinly sliced

1 tsp palm sugar or soft brown sugar

1 Tbsp Thai fish sauce or nuoc mam

3 ounces egg noodles

½ cup canned straw mushrooms (drained weight)

Heat the oil in a wok or saucepan and fry the meat, onion, and celery until the meat is cooked through and the vegetables are tender.

Add the broth, coriander (cilantro), kaffir lime leaves, ginger, sugar, and fish sauce. Bring to a boil, then add the noodles and the straw mushrooms. Cook for 10 minutes or until the noodles are tender. Serve piping hot.

Time: Preparation takes 15 minutes, cooking takes 20 minutes.

Cook's Tip: Partially freeze the beef to make slicing easier but ensure the beef is defrosted before cooking. All the ingredients can be purchased at oriental food stores.

Bean Soup

This hearty dish is as much a stew as a soup.

SERVES 4-6

14-ounce can red kidney beans

2 slices bacon, rind removed, chopped

1 stick celery, chopped

1 small onion, chopped

1 clove garlic, finely chopped

1 Tbsp chopped fresh parsley

1 Tbsp chopped fresh basil

⅔ cup canned plum tomatoes, seeded and chopped

1 quart chicken broth

Salt and freshly ground black pepper

1 cup whole-wheat pasta shapes

Put the kidney beans, bacon, celery, onion, garlic, parsley, basil, tomatoes, and broth in a large pan. Bring to a boil and add salt and pepper to taste. Cover and simmer for about 1½ hours.

Return the soup to a boil and add the pasta shapes, stirring well. Stir frequently for about 10 minutes or until the pasta is *al dente*. Check seasoning and serve immediately.

Time: Preparation takes 10 minutes, cooking takes about 1 hour 45 minutes.

Curried Meatball & Noodle Soup

Oriental noodle soups often contain meatballs. Chop the shallots for the meatballs very finely to prevent the meatballs from breaking up during cooking.

SERVES 4

Meatballs

8 ounces twice-ground lean beef

2 shallots, finely chopped

Pinch of salt and freshly ground black pepper

1 tsp cornstarch

1 egg white

Soup

2 Tbsps oil

3 shallots, finely chopped

1 clove garlic, finely chopped

1 Tbsp curry powder

1 carrot, sliced

5 cups broth

3 ounces Chinese egg noodles

Salt and freshly ground black pepper

Half a head of Chinese (Napa) cabbage, shredded

Garnish

Chopped macadamia nuts

Coriander (cilantro) leaves

Place all the ingredients for the meatballs in a large mixing bowl and mix together well. Shape into 1-inch balls and chill until ready to use.

Heat the oil for the soup in a heavy-based saucepan and add the shallots, garlic, and curry powder. Cook gently until the shallots soften. Add the carrot and broth. Partially cover the pan and bring the broth to a boil. Simmer for 15 minutes then add the meatballs. Simmer for 5-7 minutes or until the meatballs are cooked.

Add the Chinese noodles and cook about 5 minutes, or until just tender. Add salt and pepper and the Chinese cabbage. Cook for a further 5 minutes or until the leaves are tender-crisp. Spoon the soup into individual bowls and garnish with the chopped nuts and whole coriander leaves.

Time: Preparation takes 20 minutes, plus chilling time. Cooking takes about 40 minutes.

Thick Chicken Noodle Soup

This is a very meaty and substantial soup. Add more water or broth if you prefer a thinner, less filling soup.

SERVES 6

1 chicken weighing about 3 pounds
2 carrots, chopped
1 leek, sliced
2 ounces vermicelli
1 Tbsp freshly chopped mixed herbs
Salt and freshly ground black pepper

Joint the chicken and place the pieces in a large pan with sufficient water to cover. Add the chopped vegetables and bring to a boil. Cover the pan and simmer for 1 hour.

Strain the broth and return it to the pan. Bone the chicken, shred the meat, and return it to the broth. Bring to a boil and add the vermicelli, herbs, and seasonings. Simmer for 15 minutes, adding extra water if necessary. Season to taste and serve.
Time: Preparation takes 25 minutes, cooking takes 1 hour 20 minutes.

Cabbage & Pasta Soup

Cabbage soups are very popular in France; this one has a very definite Italian flavor.

SERVES 4

6 leaves white cabbage
1 Tbsp olive oil
1 clove garlic, chopped
1 strip fat bacon, cut into small dice
3¾ cups chicken broth
Salt and freshly ground black pepper
5 ounces small pasta shells

Roll the cabbage leaves into cigar shapes and shred thinly. Heat the olive oil in a large skillet and fry the garlic, bacon, and cabbage together for 2 minutes.

Add the broth, season with salt and pepper, and cook over a moderate heat for 30 minutes, adding the pasta shells halfway through cooking. Check the seasoning and serve.
Time: Preparation takes 5 minutes, cooking takes 35 minutes.
Variation: Leave the bacon whole and remove it just before serving the soup.

Shrimp & Noodle Soup

The tofu in this unusual fish soup provides plenty of protein and makes the soup almost a complete meal in itself.

SERVES 4

1 small bunch green onions (scallions)

¾ cup raw shrimp

1 bay leaf

1 small piece fresh root ginger, peeled

2 garlic cloves, peeled

1 Tbsp crushed coriander (cilantro) seeds

5 cups water

¼ tsp turmeric

1 red chili seeded and cut into very thin, short strips

1¼ cups coconut milk

6 ounces Chinese noodles, soaked 5 minutes in hot water

1 cup tofu, drained and cut into ½-inch cubes

¾ cup beansprouts

Salt

Lemon juice

Cut the green tops off the green onions (scallions) and set aside. Place the white part of the onions, shrimp, bay leaf, whole pieces of ginger and garlic, coriander (cilantro) seeds and water in a deep saucepan. Bring to a boil and simmer just until the shrimp turn pink.

Remove the shrimp with a slotted spoon and peel them. Return the shrimp shells to the broth in the pan and simmer for a further 15-20 minutes.

Chop the shrimp flesh and set it aside. Strain the broth and return to the rinsed-out pan. Add the turmeric, chili, and coconut milk. Bring to a boil, add the noodles, and simmer until completely cooked. Slice the green tops of the green onions (scallions) thinly and add to the broth with the cubed tofu, beansprouts, and the chopped shrimp. Add salt and lemon juice to taste and simmer until all the ingredients are hot.

Time: Preparation takes 15 minutes, cooking takes about 30 minutes.

Chicken & Vegetable Soup with Curry

Take care when seasoning this delicious Thai soup – macadamia nuts can be very salty and little or no extra seasoning may be required.

SERVES 4

2 pounds chicken joints

1 Tbsp curry leaves

2 Tbsps oil

4 shallots, coarsely chopped

1 clove garlic, finely chopped

1 red or green chili, seeded and finely chopped

2 tsps mild curry powder

1 small piece fresh root ginger, grated

2 tbsps macadamia nuts, chopped

3 ounces Chinese egg noodles, softened for 5 minutes in hot water

2 zucchini, diced

Juice of 1 lime

Salt

Garnish

Thin slices of lime

Place the chicken and curry leaves in a deep pan and cover with water. Simmer, partially covered, for 30-45 minutes, until the chicken is tender. Skim the surface of the liquid while the chicken cooks.

Heat the oil in a pan, add the shallots and garlic, and cook until slightly softened. Add the chili, curry powder, and ginger and cook for 2 minutes. Add the nuts and set aside.

When the chicken is cooked, remove it from the liquid and allow to cool. Strain and reserve the broth. Remove the skin and bones from the chicken and cut the meat into small pieces.

Add the chicken meat and cooked shallots, garlic, spices, and nuts to the strained broth. Bring to a boil and add the noodles and zucchini. Simmer to cook the noodles completely, and add lime juice and salt, if necessary. Garnish with lime slices and serve.

Time: Preparation takes 30 minutes, cooking takes 1 hour.

Appetizers

Appetizers are usually reserved for company, so they really need to be special. We think you will find the selection in this section of the book lives up to that expectation. Here are appetizers which combine pasta with lox (smoked salmon), seafood, and even fish roe and escargots. Vegetarians will appreciate Fresh Pasta with Ceps, and Pasta with Basil and Walnut Sauce, but you don't have to be a vegetarian to enjoy these delicious combinations.

Small pasta shapes can also be used as stuffings. We include recipes for Stuffed Tomatoes and Stuffed Zucchini. The quantities could be increased and used to stuff a squash or even a pumpkin. Baked stuffed squash or pumpkin makes a great dish for a buffet.

Appetizers containing pasta can be served hot or cold. A hot appetizer is much appreciated in the cooler months as an interesting alternative to soup, and pasta has the advantage of being so quick and easy to cook or re-heat. Most of the dishes in this section can be prepared in advance and reheated on the stovetop or in the microwave just before serving. Several of these dishes make great cocktail snacks, particularly the Pork Wrapped in Noodles (page 31) and the Stuffed Tomatoes (page 35).

Contrasting, brightly colored pastas do not need the addition of elaborate and expensive ingredients. They look best cooked simply and tossed in butter and plenty of freshly grated Parmesan cheese, as in our recipe for Fettuccini with Butter and Cheese (page 32) which uses tricolored noodles. Simply cooked pasta should always be served freshly cooked and really hot. Always buy Parmesan cheese in the largest piece you can afford and grate it at home. Keep the cheese in an airtight container in the refrigerator. You can grate cheese in advance, provided you keep it in the refrigerator in a sealed bag, but it is best grated fresh each time you intend to serve it.

Pasta used in cold dishes should be cooked at least two hours in advance and rinsed thoroughly after cooking, so that the pieces do not stick together. It should then be allowed to cool completely, especially if it is used for stuffing.

Stuffed Zucchini

Stuffed zucchini make an elegant appetizer. Be careful to choose even-sized zucchini for this dish.

SERVES 4

½ cup small pasta shapes for soup
4 zucchini
2 Tbsps butter or margarine
2 garlic cloves, finely chopped
1 small onion, chopped
½ pound ground beef
1 tsp tomato paste
Salt and freshly ground black pepper
2 tomatoes, skinned, seeded, and chopped
¼ cup grated fontina cheese
1 Tbsp fresh bread crumbs

Cook the pasta in plenty of boiling, salted water for 5 minutes, or until *al dente*. Rinse in cold water and drain well.

Meanwhile, place the zucchini in a pan and cover with cold water. Bring to a boil and cook gently for 3 minutes. Rinse under cold water. Cut the zucchini in half lengthwise, and carefully scoop out the pulp, leaving a ½-inch shell. Chop the pulp.

Heat the butter in a skillet. Add the garlic and onion and sauté gently until transparent. Increase the heat and add the ground beef. Fry for 5 minutes, stirring frequently, until the meat is well browned. Stir in the tomato paste and add salt and pepper. Add the zucchini pulp, tomatoes, and pasta and cook for 2 minutes.

Spoon the mixture into the zucchini shells and top with a layer of the grated cheese and bread crumbs. Brown under a broiler and serve immediately.

Time: Preparation takes 15 minutes, cooking takes 30 minutes.

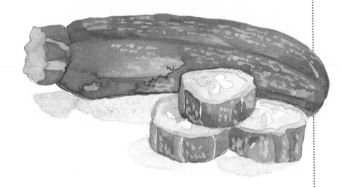

Shell Pasta with Taramasalata

Home-made taramasalata is delicious – used as a sauce for freshly cooked pasta it is rich and most unusual.

SERVES 4

Taramasalata

8 thick slices white bread, crusts removed

4 Tbsps milk

8 ounces smoked cod's roe

Half an onion, grated

⅓ cup olive oil

2 Tbsps lemon juice

Freshly ground black pepper

To serve

8 ounces pasta shells

2 Tbsps lemon juice

1 Tbsp caviar or black lumpfish roe

10 black olives, pitted and chopped

To make the taramasalata, crumble the bread into a bowl and add the milk. Set aside to soak. Scoop the cod's roe out of the skin or jar, and break it down with a wooden spoon. Squeeze the bread dry in a strainer. Add the onion and bread to the roe and mix well. Add the oil and lemon juice very gradually, alternating between the two. Beat until smooth and creamy. Add pepper to taste, and salt if necessary.

Cook the pasta shells in plenty of boiling, salted water for 10-12 minutes or until *al dente*. Rinse in hot water and drain well. Sprinkle the lemon juice over the pasta and toss with the taramasalata. Garnish with the caviar or lumpfish roe and chopped black olives. Serve immediately.

Time: Preparation takes 15 minutes, cooking takes 15 minutes.

Cook's Tip: If smoked cod's roe is not available use other smoked roe, such as whitefish.

Fettuccini with Cream & Mushrooms

Dried mushrooms have a very intense flavor. If you wish to tone down the flavor use a mixture of dried and fresh mushrooms.

SERVES 6

3 Tbsps dried or 2 cups fresh mushrooms
3 Tbsps olive oil
1 medium onion, chopped
1 pound fettuccini
½ cup light cream
2 Tbsps grated Parmesan cheese
2 Tbsps chopped fresh parsley
Salt and freshly ground black pepper

Soak the dried mushrooms in water for 2-3 hours. Drain and squeeze out the liquid, then chop the mushrooms roughly. Heat the oil in a small skillet and sauté the chopped onion for 1-2 minutes. Add the mushrooms to the pan and cook for 10 minutes.

Meanwhile, cook the fettuccini in plenty of boiling, salted water for 10-12 minutes, or until *al dente*. Drain and return the pasta to the pan. Stir in the mushrooms, cream, Parmesan and parsley. Season well and stir until heated through and well mixed. Serve at once.

Time: Preparation takes 10 minutes, plus soaking time. Cooking takes about 20 minutes.

Pasta with Basil & Walnut Sauce

This is a classic sauce for pasta – try it once and you'll be convinced!

SERVES 6

½ cup walnut meats
15 fresh basil leaves
1 small clove garlic
1 pound pasta
Olive oil
4 Tbsps butter
Salt and freshly ground black pepper

Pound together the walnuts, basil, and garlic in a mortar with a pestle, until a smooth paste is formed. Cook the pasta in boiling, salted water for 10-12 minutes, or until *al dente*. Rinse in hot water and set aside to drain.

Heat a little olive oil and the butter together in a pan, add the basil, walnut, and garlic paste and stir well. Add the pasta to the pan, stir well, and heat through. Add salt and pepper as necessary. Serve immediately.

Time: Preparation takes 10 minutes, cooking takes 15 minutes.

Shellfish in Egg Noodle Nests

A perfect dish to make a big impression on guests! The clams and mussels may be replaced by shrimp or any other shellfish.

SERVES 4-6

4 ounces Chinese egg noodles

24 mussels, washed and thoroughly rinsed

1 cup clams, washed and thoroughly rinsed

1 cup Chinese wine

1 small zucchini

Oil for deep-frying

1 Tbsp oil

1 clove garlic, finely chopped

½ tsp finely chopped fresh root ginger

2 leaves Chinese (Napa) cabbage, shredded

1½ tsps soy sauce

1½ tsps oyster sauce

Salt and freshly ground black pepper

Cook the egg noodles in boiling, lightly salted water until just tender. Rinse under cold water and set aside to drain.

Discard any mussels or clams with broken shells or those that do not shut when lightly tapped. Cook the mussels and clams with the wine in a large, covered saucepan for 3-5 minutes, until the shells have opened, then remove them from their shells. Discard any shells that have not opened. Thickly peel the zucchini and slice the skin into thin matchsticks. Discard the central flesh and seeds.

Heat some oil in a deep-fat fryer to 350 degrees. Make the noodle nests by placing a few noodles on the inside of a small basket fryer or a metal draining spoon. Clamp the noodles in place with a second basket or draining spoon. Plunge each nest into the hot oil and cook for 1-2 minutes, until golden-brown and crisp. Remove the nest and drain it on absorbent kitchen paper. Repeat the process with the remaining noodles.

Heat the 1 Tbsp oil in a wok and stir-fry the garlic, ginger, clams, mussels, and Chinese (Napa) cabbage for 1 minute. Stir in the soy and oyster sauces and season to taste with salt and pepper. Allow the liquid to reduce slightly. Divide the mixture evenly between the noodle nests.

Time: Preparation takes 20 minutes, cooking takes about 15 minutes.

Fettuccini, Leeks & Sun-dried Tomatoes

Canned snails are delicious in dishes such as this, where they are flavored with garlic, mushrooms, and sun-dried tomatoes.

SERVES 4-6

6 sun-dried tomatoes
14-ounce can escargots (snails)
12 ounces fresh or dried whole-wheat fettuccini
3 Tbsps olive oil
2 garlic cloves, finely chopped
1 large or 2 small leeks, trimmed and finely sliced
6 oyster or other large mushrooms, sliced
4 Tbsps chicken or vegetable broth
3 Tbsps dry white wine
6 Tbsps heavy cream
1 Tbsp chopped fresh basil
1 Tbsp chopped fresh parsley
Salt and freshly ground black pepper

Chop the sun-dried tomatoes roughly. Drain the escargots well and dry on absorbent kitchen paper.

Place the fettuccini in a large pan of boiling, salted water and cook for 12-15 minutes, or until *al dente*. Drain, rinse under hot water, and leave in a colander to drain again.

Meanwhile, heat the olive oil in a skillet and add the garlic and leeks. Cook slowly until just starting to soften, then add the mushrooms and cook until the leeks are just slightly crisp. Transfer the vegetables to a plate.

Add the drained escargots to the pan and cook over a high heat for about 2 minutes, stirring constantly. Add the broth and wine, and bring to a boil. Boil to reduce by about a quarter, then add the cream and the sun-dried tomatoes. Bring to a boil then cook slowly for about 3 minutes.

Add the herbs and salt and pepper to taste. Add the leeks, mushroom mixture, and fettuccini to the pan and heat through. Serve immediately.

Time: Preparation takes about 10 minutes, cooking takes 20 minutes.

Variation: Snails are not to everyone's taste, so substitute more mushrooms, cooked shrimp, or spicy sausage if desired.

Fettuccini with Lox

This is affordable luxury! You can use white or green pasta, or a mixture of the two.

SERVES 4

8 ounces green or white fettuccini
2 Tbsps butter or margarine
Juice of ½ lemon
Freshly ground black pepper
3 slices lox (smoked salmon), cut into strips
2 Tbsps heavy cream
2 Tbsps salmon roe or lumpfish roe
Lemon slices

Cook the fettuccini in plenty of boiling, salted water for 10-12 minutes, or until *al dente*. Rinse under hot water and drain well.

Heat the butter in a pan, add the lemon juice and some freshly ground black pepper, then add the fettuccini and lox, and toss together. Top with the heavy cream and the salmon roe or lumpfish roe. Garnish with lemon slices.

Time: Preparation takes 5 minutes, cooking takes 15 minutes.

Cook's Tip: Ensure the fettuccini is well drained or it will water down the butter sauce.

Pork Wrapped in — Noodles —

This makes a delicious and original appetizer or cocktail snack.

SERVES 4

1 cup twice-ground pork
1 tsp ground coriander (cilantro)
1 Tbsp fish sauce (nuoc mam)
1 small egg, beaten
3 ounces vermicelli
Oil for deep-frying
Whole chilies, to garnish

Mix together the pork, coriander (cilantro), and fish sauce, then add enough egg to bind the mixture together. Roll the mixture into small balls and chill for 30 minutes.

Cover the noodles with warm water and soak for about 10 minutes to soften. Drain the noodles, then wrap several strands around each pork ball.

Heat the oil in a wok and deep-fry a few of the meatballs at a time for 3-4 minutes, or until crisp and golden. Drain on kitchen paper. Garnish with whole chilies.

Time: Preparation takes 15 minutes, plus chilling time. Cooking takes about 20 minutes.

Serving Idea: Serve with a hot dipping sauce.

Macaroni with Olive Sauce

Make this dish with green or black olives, or a mixture of both.

SERVES 4

12 ounces macaroni

4 Tbsps butter

1 clove garlic, finely chopped

10 olives, pitted and finely chopped

Salt and freshly ground black pepper

Cook the macaroni in boiling, salted water for 10-12 minutes, or until *al dente*. Rinse in hot water and set aside to drain.

Melt the butter in a saucepan and add the garlic and olives. Cook for 1 minute and then stir in the macaroni. Check the seasoning, adding salt and pepper as necessary. Serve hot.

Time: Preparation takes 5 minutes, cooking takes about 15 minutes.

Variation: Add some capers, but reduce the added salt.

Fettuccini with Butter & Cheese

This recipe is simple, yet wickedly delicious.

SERVES 4

10 ounces tri-colored fettuccini

⅓ cup butter

⅓ cup heavy cream

4 Tbsps grated Parmesan cheese

Salt and freshly ground black pepper

Cook the fettuccini in a large saucepan of boiling, salted water for 10-12 minutes, or until *al dente*. Drain well.

Meanwhile, place the butter and cream in a pan and stir over a low heat until the butter has melted. Remove from the heat, add half the grated Parmesan cheese, and salt and pepper to taste. Stir into the drained fettuccini and serve immediately with the remaining Parmesan cheese sprinkled on top.

Time: Preparation takes 5 minutes, cooking takes 15 minutes.

Pasta-stuffed Cabbage Leaves

Use a small soup pasta for the stuffing in this recipe, or the cabbage leaves will not roll up easily around the mixture.

SERVES 4

4 ounces small pasta shapes

Salt

8-12 large cabbage leaves, washed

1 hard cooked egg, finely chopped

4 Tbsps walnuts, chopped

1 Tbsp chopped fresh chives

2 Tbsps chopped fresh parsley

1 tsp chopped fresh marjoram

Freshly ground black pepper

1¼ cups vegetable broth

1 Tbsp walnut oil

1 onion, finely chopped

1 green bell pepper, chopped

14-ounce can chopped tomatoes

1 cup button mushrooms, chopped

2 Tbsps tomato paste

1 bayleaf

Pinch of sugar

Cook the pasta in plenty of boiling, salted water for 8 minutes or until *al dente*. Remove the thick stems from the base of the cabbage leaves. Blanch the leaves in boiling water for 3 minutes, then drain and refresh them in cold water.

When the pasta is cooked, drain it well and mix with the egg, walnuts, herbs, and a little pepper. Divide the pasta mixture between the cabbage leaves, fold up to completely enclose the filling, and secure with cocktail sticks. Place the cabbage rolls in a shallow ovenproof dish and add the broth. Cover and bake in a oven preheated to 350 degrees for 40 minutes.

Heat the oil in a skillet and fry the onion and pepper for 5 minutes, or until soft. Stir in the tomatoes, mushrooms, tomato paste, bayleaf, and sugar. Season to taste and cook gently for 10 minutes. Remove the cabbage parcels from the casserole dish with a slotted spoon and serve with the sauce poured over them.

Time: Preparation takes 15 minutes, cooking takes about 50 minutes.

Pasta Shells with Agliata Sauce

The good thing about pasta shells is that they trap pools of sauce inside them, making wonderful mouthfuls of flavor.

SERVES 4

10 ounces whole-wheat pasta shells
Salt and freshly ground black pepper

Sauce

6 Tbsps olive oil
3 Tbsps fresh parsley, roughly chopped
2 garlic cloves, roughly chopped
1 Tbsp pine nuts
1 Tbsp blanched almonds

Cook the pasta shells in a large pan of boiling, salted water for 12-15 minutes, or until *al dente*.

Meanwhile, make the sauce. Place all the ingredients in a blender or food processor and blend until smooth. Add salt and pepper to taste. Drain the hot, cooked pasta shells and toss together with the prepared sauce. Serve immediately.

Time: Preparation takes 5 minutes, cooking takes 12-15 minutes.

Fettuccini with Eggs — & Caviar —

This dish is light and sophisticated – add a splash of vodka just before serving for special occasions.

SERVES 4

4 small eggs, hard cooked
8 ounces red fettuccini
4 Tbsps butter or margarine
Freshly ground black pepper
4 Tbsps salmon roe or lumpfish roe

Remove the shells from the hard-cooked eggs, cut the eggs in half, and scoop out the yolks with a teaspoon. Press the yolks through a strainer. Wash the egg whites and cut them into strips.

Cook the fettuccini in plenty of boiling, salted water for 10-12 minutes, or until *al dente*. Rinse in hot water and drain well.

Heat the butter in a pan, add some freshly ground black pepper and the fettuccini. Add the egg whites and toss well. Sprinkle the salmon or lumpfish roe over and top with the sieved egg yolks. Serve immediately.

Time: Preparation takes 10 minutes, cooking takes 15 minutes.

Stuffed Tomatoes

Use large, beefsteak tomatoes for this recipe.

SERVES 4

4 large ripe tomatoes

1 pound fresh spinach

2 ounces small pasta shapes

2 Tbsps butter, softened

1 Tbsp heavy cream

¼ tsp grated nutmeg

1 clove garlic, finely chopped

Salt and freshly ground black pepper

1 Tbsp grated Parmesan or Cheddar cheese

4 anchovy fillets, halved lengthwise

Cut the tops off the tomatoes and carefully scoop out the insides with a teaspoon. Wash the spinach well in lots of water and remove the stalks. Put the spinach in a large saucepan and cook gently, without any added water, until it is soft. Chop the spinach very finely or purée in a blender or food processor.

Squeeze well in a clean cloth or between two plates to remove all the excess moisture.

Meanwhile, cook the pasta in plenty of boiling water for 8 minutes, or until *al dente*. Rinse and drain well, then mix with the spinach. Add the butter, cream, nutmeg, and garlic, and season well.

Fill each tomato with the spinach mixture and top with the grated cheese. Arrange the anchovies on top. Place in an ovenproof dish and bake in an oven preheated to 400 degrees for 10-12 minutes. Serve immediately.

Time: Preparation takes 10 minutes, cooking takes about 20 minutes.

Pasta with Clams

Any type of clams will do as long as they are raw and in their shells. If clams are not available, use mussels.

SERVES 4

2 cups raw clams, scrubbed
½ cup dry white wine
1 shallot, chopped
11 ounces spaghetti or linguini
4 Tbsps butter
1 clove garlic, chopped
1 Tbsp chopped fresh parsley
Salt and freshly ground black pepper

Scrub the clams under running water. Discard any with broken shells or those that do not shut when lightly tapped.

Place the clams in a large pan, add the white wine and shallot, and place over a high heat for 4-5 minutes, or until the clams have opened. Shake the pan frequently. Remove from the heat and set the pan aside until the clams are cool enough to handle, then remove them from their shells. Discard any that have not opened.

Cook the pasta in plenty of boiling, salted water for 10-12 minutes, or until *al dente*. Rinse in hot water and set aside to drain. Melt the butter in a pan, add the garlic, chopped parsley, pasta, and the clams. Season with salt and pepper. Cook until the pasta is heated through. Serve immediately.

Time: Preparation takes 10 minutes, cooking takes 20 minutes.

Fettuccini with Pine Nuts

This is a piquant recipe, suitable for vegetarians, but popular with meat eaters too! The pine nuts give a slightly crunchy texture to the dish.

SERVES 4

12 ounces fettuccini

6 Tbsps olive oil

1 large onion, sliced

1 clove garlic, finely chopped

½ cup pine nuts

14-ounce can artichoke hearts, drained

2 Tbsps chopped fresh parsley

Parmesan cheese, grated

Cook the fettuccini in plenty of lightly salted boiling water for 10-12 minutes, or until *al dente*. Just before the fettuccini is cooked, heat the oil in a skillet and fry the onion and garlic until starting to brown. Add the pine nuts and cook for 1 minute, then add the artichoke hearts and parsley. Heat gently for a few minutes. Drain the pasta well and add it to the pan; toss until the fettuccini are well coated in the oil. Stir in a generous handful of grated Parmesan. Transfer to a warmed serving dish and scatter with a little more grated Parmesan. Serve immediately.

Time: Preparation takes 5 minutes, cooking takes 15 minutes.

Salads & Light Meals

Cold pasta salads were the latest food fad a few years ago. Gourmet food stores were stocked with a variety of pasta salads, all drenched in oil, and mostly featuring dried basil and the inevitable sun-dried tomatoes. A surfeit of pasta salads caused them to lose popularity for a while.

We hope that this section will tempt you back into pasta salads and show you what a wide variety of tastes, flavors, and textures you can create using pasta. Pasta turns a salad into a hearty side-dish or even a complete meal, making it a convenient and healthy option for dieters. We have also included a few "light meals," pasta dishes which can be eaten as a snack such as Pasta and Vegetables in Parmesan Dressing (page 45) and Chinese Noodles with Vegetables (page 47).

Pasta salads are particularly suitable as side dishes at a barbecue. They go well with the barbecued meats but are satisfying and interesting enough to serve to vegetarians and anyone else who would rather not eat large quantities of the broiled meats. Pasta salads are also a good idea for pot-luck dinners when you can't think of a dish to take along.

Home-made mayonnaise is best in pasta salads and you can vary the flavorings when you make it yourself. Mayonnaise is very easy to make in a blender. If you are wary of using raw eggs, as required in classic mayonnaise recipes, substitute two tablespoons of tofu per egg. Slimmers can replace the mayonnaise which is an ingredient in so many cold pasta dishes with low-fat yogurt and low-fat sour cream substitute. However, there are also salads in this section, such as Mushroom Pasta Salad (page 43) and Pasta and Asparagus Salad (page 41) which contain no mayonnaise and very little oil. The oil could be reduced by half, to make them into good dishes for dieters. If the vegetables are boiled or steamed in a little broth instead of being stir-fried, then added to noodles, they make a nourishing light meal.

Bean Salad

Crispy bacon adds flavor and texture to this bean and pasta salad.

SERVES 4

8 ounces macaroni
2 slices lean bacon, rind removed, chopped
1 onion, chopped
1-2 Tbsps wine vinegar
3-4 Tbsps olive oil
1 tsp chopped fresh parsley
Salt and freshly ground black pepper
14-ounce can red kidney beans, drained
2 sticks celery, sliced diagonally

Cook the macaroni in plenty of salted, boiling water for 10 minutes, or until *al dente*. Rinse in cold water and drain well. Heat a skillet and sauté the bacon in its own fat until crisp. Add the onion and cook until soft.

Mix together the vinegar, oil, and parsley, and season well. Add the bacon-and-onion mixture, the kidney beans, and celery to the macaroni. Pour the dressing over the salad and toss together well. Chill briefly before serving.

Time: Preparation takes 10 minutes, cooking takes 15 minutes.

Cook's Tip: Use a red onion for a more subtle flavor.

Niçoise Salad

A variation on the classic version of this delicious salad.

SERVES 4

8 ounces penne
7 ounces canned tuna, drained and flaked
3 tomatoes, quartered
½ cucumber, cut into batons
½ cup cooked green beans
12 black olives, pitted and halved
2-ounce can anchovy fillets, soaked in milk then drained
Salt and freshly ground black pepper
½ cup French dressing

Cook the penne in plenty of boiling, salted water for 10-12 minutes, or until *al dente*. Rinse in cold water, drain and leave to dry.

Place the flaked tuna in the bottom of a salad bowl. Add the cooked pasta, tomatoes, cucumber, beans, olives, and anchovies, and toss together well. Add salt and pepper to taste. Pour the French dressing over the salad and mix together well.

Time: Preparation takes 15 minutes, cooking takes 15 minutes.

Cook's Tip: Soaking the anchovy fillets in milk removes any excess saltiness.

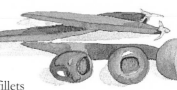

Pasta & Asparagus Salad

This makes an elegant summer salad.

SERVES 4

4 ounces fettuccini or pasta shapes

1 pound bunch fresh green asparagus

2 zucchini

2 Tbsps chopped fresh parsley and 2 Tbsps chopped fresh marjoram

1 lemon, peel and white parts removed, flesh segmented

Grated rind and juice of 1 lemon

⅓ cup olive oil

Pinch of sugar

Salt and freshly ground black pepper

Crisp lettuce and frisée leaves

Cook the pasta in plenty of boiling, salted water for 10-12 minutes, or until *al dente*. Drain and refresh in cold water. Drain again and leave to cool completely.

Trim the woody sections of the asparagus stems. Cut the asparagus into 1-inch lengths. Cut the zucchini into 2-inch sections, then into batons. Cook the asparagus in lightly salted, boiling water for 4 minutes, then add the zucchini and cook for 3-4 minutes, until just tender. Drain and refresh in cold water. Drain again and leave to cool.

Place the pasta, vegetables, herbs, and lemon segments in a large bowl. Mix together the lemon rind and juice, oil, sugar, and some salt and pepper to make the dressing. Arrange the lettuce and frisée on serving plates. Just before serving, pour the dressing over the vegetables and pasta and toss to coat well. Pile the pasta salad into the center of the salad leaves and serve immediately.
Time: Preparation takes 15 minutes. Cooking takes 20 minutes.

Mexican Chicken Salad

This simple salad is perfect for picnics.

SERVES 4

8 ounces small pasta shapes for soup

1 Tbsp mayonnaise

2 Tbsps white wine vinegar

Salt and freshly ground black pepper

1 cup shredded cooked chicken

1 cup canned corn kernels, drained

1 stick celery, sliced

1 red bell pepper, diced

1 green bell pepper, diced

Cook the pasta in plenty of boiling, salted water for 8 minutes, or until *al dente*. Drain well and leave to cool.

Meanwhile, combine the mayonnaise with the vinegar and salt and pepper to make a dressing. When the pasta is cool, add the chicken, corn, celery, and peppers. Toss together well and serve with the dressing.
Time: Preparation takes 10 minutes, cooking takes 15 minutes.
Variation: Add some chili sauce to the dressing instead of vinegar for a spicier flavor.

Gianfottere Salad

A pasta salad that celebrates summer vegetables.

SERVES 4

1 small eggplant

2 tomatoes

1 large zucchini

1 red bell pepper

1 green bell pepper

1 medium onion

1 clove garlic

4 Tbsps olive oil

Salt and freshly ground black pepper

1 pound whole-wheat pasta spirals or bows

Cut the eggplant into ½-inch slices, then cubes. Chop the tomatoes roughly and remove the woody cores. Cut the zucchini into ½-inch slices. Seed the peppers and chop them roughly. Chop the onion and crush the garlic.

Heat 3 Tbsps of the olive oil in a skillet and cook the onion gently until it is transparent but not colored. Stir the eggplant into the onion along with the zucchini, peppers, tomatoes, and garlic. Fry gently for 20 minutes. Season with salt and pepper to taste, then leave until completely cool.

Cook the pasta spirals in plenty of boiling, salted water for 10-12 minutes, or until *al dente*. Rinse in cold water and drain well. Place the pasta spirals in a large bowl, and stir in the remaining olive oil. Stir the vegetables into the pasta and adjust the seasoning if necessary. Chill before serving.

Time: Preparation takes 15 minutes, cooking takes 30 minutes.

Variation: Substitute sliced mushrooms for the eggplant.

Shrimp Salad

This recipe makes a very quick lunch dish for two or an appetizer for four.

SERVES 2-4

8 ounces pasta shells

Juice of 1 lemon

1 tsp paprika

⅔ cup mayonnaise

1 cup cooked bay shrimp, shelled and deveined

Salt and freshly ground black pepper

1 lettuce

1 cucumber, sliced

Cook the pasta in plenty of boiling, salted water for 10-12 minutes, or until *al dente*. Drain and rinse under cold water. Shake off any excess water, then place the pasta in a bowl, and add the lemon juice. Leave to cool.

Mix the paprika into the mayonnaise and add the shrimp and salt and pepper, then mix gently. Arrange a bed of lettuce leaves and sliced cucumber in a dish and pile the pasta into the center with the shrimp on top.

Time: Preparation takes 10 minutes, cooking takes 15 minutes.

Variation: Substitute flaked crabmeat or salmon for the shrimp. Garnish with a few shelled and deveined jumbo shrimp.

Mushroom Pasta Salad

Add a clove or two of crushed garlic to this salad if you wish.

SERVES 4

5 Tbsps olive oil
Juice of 2 lemons
1 Tbsp chopped fresh basil
1 Tbsp chopped fresh parsley
Salt and freshly ground black pepper
2 cups mushrooms, finely sliced
8 ounces whole-wheat pasta shapes

Whisk together the olive oil, lemon juice, herbs, and salt and pepper in a large bowl. Add the mushrooms to the lemon dressing and stir well to coat the mushrooms evenly. Cover the bowl and leave to marinate in a cool place for at least 1 hour.

Cook the pasta in a large pan of boiling, salted water for 12-15 minutes, or until *al dente*. Rinse the pasta in cold water and drain well. Add the pasta to the marinated mushrooms and lemon dressing, mixing well to coat the pasta shapes evenly. Adjust the seasoning if necessary, then chill well before serving.

Time: Preparation takes 10 minutes, plus 1 hour for the mushrooms to marinate. Cooking takes 15 minutes.

Variation: Use a mixture of button and wild mushrooms for a stronger flavor.

Chicken & Grape Pasta Salad

Chicken and grapes complement each other perfectly. Grapes are the classic garnish for Coronation Chicken, on which this recipe is based.

SERVES 4-6

12 ounces pasta spirals or bows
1-2 Tbsps olive oil
1 onion, finely chopped
1 cup shredded cooked chicken
1 red bell pepper, finely chopped
½ cup seedless green grapes
½ cup black grapes, deseeded
⅔ cup mayonnaise
⅔ cup plain yogurt
1-2 tsps curry paste
Salt and freshly ground black pepper
Chopped fresh coriander (cilantro) to garnish

Cook the pasta in plenty of boiling, salted water for 10-12 minutes, or until *al dente*. Drain, then rinse in cold water and drain again. Leave until cold.

Heat the olive oil in a small skillet, add the onion, and cook gently for 3-4 minutes until softened. Allow to cool.

Mix together the chicken and pepper. Cut the grapes in half lengthwise if they are large and add them to the chicken with the cold cooked pasta and onion. Mix together the mayonnaise and yogurt and add curry paste to taste. Season the salad with salt and pepper, then pour the dressing over it and toss until the pasta is well coated. Chill until required. Garnish with coriander (cilantro) just before serving.

Time: Preparation takes 10 minutes, cooking takes about 15 minutes.

Fisherman's Whole-wheat Pasta Salad

Other seafood or canned tuna can be used as a variation.

SERVES 4

8 ounces whole-wheat pasta shapes

Salt and freshly ground black pepper

4 Tbsps olive oil

2 Tbsps dry white wine

1 Tbsp minced fresh parsley

3 green onions (scallions), chopped

½ cup cooked, shelled mussels

⅔ cup peeled bay shrimp

½ cup shredded crabmeat

12 pitted black olives

4 whole jumbo shrimp, to garnish

Cook the pasta in a large pan of boiling, salted water for 12-15 minutes, or until *al dente*.

Meanwhile, prepare the dressing. Mix the olive oil with the white wine, parsley, and salt and pepper to taste. Drain the cooked pasta thoroughly and stir in the prepared dressing. Allow to cool.

Mix in the chopped green onions (scallions) and then carefully stir in all the seafood, except the jumbo shrimp. Add the black olives, whole or halved. Spoon the salad into one large salad bowl or four individual ones. Garnish with the whole jumbo shrimp.

Time: Preparation takes 20 minutes, cooking takes about 15 minutes.

Tuna & Kidney Bean Pasta Salad

This substantial salad is suitable for serving as an entrée.

SERVES 4-6

8 ounces small pasta shells

1 cup canned red kidney beans, drained and rinsed

1 cup button mushrooms, quartered

1 cup canned tuna, drained and flaked

4 green onions (scallions), sliced

2 Tbsps chopped fresh mixed herbs

Dressing

⅔ cup olive oil

3 Tbsps white wine vinegar

Squeeze of lemon juice

1 Tbsp Dijon mustard

Salt and freshly ground black pepper

Cook the pasta shells in boiling, salted water for 10-12 minutes, or until *al dente*. Rinse under hot water and then place in cold water until ready to use.

Mix the dressing ingredients together. Drain the pasta shells. Mix the pasta with the beans, mushrooms, tuna, green onions (scallions), and chopped mixed herbs. Pour the dressing over the mixture and toss well. Chill for up to 1 hour in the refrigerator before serving.

Time: Preparation takes 15 minutes, cooking takes 10 minutes.

Cook's Tip: Do not be tempted to substitute dried herbs for the fresh herbs in this recipe; the flavor will not be the same.

Pasta & Vegetables in Parmesan Dressing

There is one problem with this recipe – the dressing is so delicious that you can eat it by itself!

SERVES 6

1 pound pasta spirals

2 cups assorted vegetables such as:

Zucchini, cut in slices or matchsticks

Broccoli, trimmed into very small flowerets

Snow peas, trimmed

Carrots, cut into slices or matchsticks

Celery, cut into matchsticks

Green onions (scallions), thinly shredded or sliced

Asparagus tips

French beans, sliced

Red or yellow peppers, thinly sliced

Cucumber, cut into matchsticks

Dressing

⅔ cup olive oil

3 Tbsps lemon juice

1 Tbsp hot pepper sauce

1 Tbsp chopped fresh parsley

1 Tbsp chopped fresh basil

4 Tbsps grated Parmesan cheese

2 Tbsps mild mustard

Salt and freshly ground black pepper

Pinch of sugar

Cook the pasta in a large pan of boiling, salted water for 10-12 minutes, or until *al dente*. Rinse under hot water then leave to stand in cold water.

Cook all the vegetables except the cucumber in boiling, salted water for 3 minutes, or until just tender. Rinse in cold water and leave to drain. Mix all the dressing ingredients together.

Place the pasta in a serving dish and toss it with the dressing. Add the vegetables and toss until coated. Refrigerate for up to 1 hour before serving.

Time: Preparation takes 25 minutes, cooking takes 15 minutes.

Serving Idea: Serve with assorted Italian meats and French bread.

Country Sauce with -Fresh Pasta-

This sauce is quick and easy to prepare from basic ingredients, a great standby for unexpected company.

SERVES 4

11 ounces pasta
1 Tbsp olive oil
1 onion, sliced
2 slices ham, cut into small pieces
6 fresh basil leaves, chopped
1 tomato, seeded and chopped
Salt and freshly ground black pepper
4 Tbsps butter
2 Tbsps grated Parmesan cheese

Cook the pasta in boiling, salted water for 10-12 minutes, or until *al dente*. Rinse under hot water and set aside to drain.

Heat the olive oil in a skillet and gently cook the onion, ham, basil, and tomato for about 20 minutes. Season with salt and pepper.

Melt the butter in a saucepan and add the pasta, stirring well. Stir in the sauce and serve when the pasta is hot. Top with the grated Parmesan and serve immediately.

Time: Preparation takes 10 minutes, cooking takes about 25 minutes.

Whole-wheat Spaghetti with -Peas & Ham-

Peas and ham in plenty of butter make a simple, tasty flavoring for pasta.

SERVES 4

10 ounces whole-wheat spaghetti
1½ cups shelled young peas
1 tsp sugar
⅓ cup butter or margarine
4 slices lean country ham, diced
Salt and freshly ground black pepper
Chopped fresh parsley (optional)

Cook the spaghetti in plenty of boiling, salted water for 12-15 minutes, or until *al dente*.

Meanwhile, cook the peas in boiling water with a pinch of salt and a teaspoon of sugar. Melt the butter in a skillet and fry the ham. When browned, add the drained peas and salt and pepper to taste.

Place the spaghetti in a serving dish and pour the peas and ham over it. Toss together well to make sure the butter coats the pasta evenly. Serve immediately, garnished with chopped parsley, if wished.

Time: Preparation takes 10 minutes, cooking takes 15 minutes.

Chinese Noodles with —Vegetables—

This pasta dish has a taste of the Orient about it.

SERVES 4

2 Tbsps dried black Chinese mushrooms (wood ears)

2 carrots

¼ cucumber

1 cup canned bamboo shoots, drained

2 Tbsps fresh beansprouts

14 ounces Chinese egg noodles

3 Tbsps oil

3 peeled slices fresh root ginger, shredded

1 clove garlic, finely chopped

1 small chili, finely chopped

5 Tbsps soy sauce

1 Tbsp honey

Salt and freshly ground black pepper

Chopped fresh chives

Soak the dried mushrooms for 15 minutes in boiling water. Drain, then discard the stalks, and boil the mushroom caps for 5 minutes. Squeeze the water from the mushrooms and slice the caps. Cut the carrots into matchsticks. Cut the cucumber into chunks. Peel the chunks thickly and discard the seeds. Cut into matchsticks. Cut the bamboo shoots into matchsticks, blanch for 2 minutes in boiling water, then drain and set aside. Wash the beansprouts, blanch for 1 minute, then plunge into cold water and drain.

Cook the noodles in boiling, salted water for a few minutes – the exact cooking time will depend on the thickness of the noodles. Drain, rinse and set aside. Heat the oil in a wok or skillet and stir-fry the ginger, garlic, and chili for a few seconds. Add the bamboo shoots, mushrooms, and carrots. Stir-fry for 4 minutes then add the beansprouts. Cook for a further 2 minutes.

Add the noodles, soy sauce, and honey. Stir well and heat through. Add the cucumber at the last moment. Heat for 1 minute then season to taste with salt and pepper. Garnish with the chives and serve.
Time: Preparation takes 20 minutes, cooking takes about 20 minutes.

Zucchini & Sweetcorn
—— Savory ——

This delicious vegetarian pasta bake is a good way of using up leftover pasta.

SERVES 4

1 Tbsp oil
1 medium onion, chopped
2 cups sliced zucchini
1 cup canned corn, drained
6 ounces pasta shapes, cooked
Large pinch of dried oregano
1 Tbsp tomato paste
Salt and freshly ground black pepper

Cheese sauce

2 Tbsps butter or margarine
2 Tbsps whole-wheat flour
1¼ cups milk
3 Tbsps dry white wine
4 Tbsps grated sharp cheese

Topping

2 Tbsps whole-wheat bread crumbs
1 Tbsp sunflower seeds

Heat the oil in a skillet and cook the chopped onion until soft. Add the sliced zucchini and brown lightly, then mix in the corn, cooked pasta shapes, oregano, and tomato paste and stir well. Season lightly and transfer the mixture to a greased ovenproof dish.

Melt the butter in a saucepan, stir in the flour, and cook gently for a few seconds. Gradually add the milk and wine, stirring all the time, to make a smooth sauce. Bring gently to a boil, stirring constantly, then simmer for 1-2 minutes. Add the grated cheese and stir until it melts into the sauce. Remove the pan from the heat and pour the sauce over the vegetables.

Mix the topping ingredients together and scatter evenly over the dish. Bake in an oven, preheated to 350 degrees, for about 20 minutes, or until browned and bubbling. Time: Preparation takes 10 minutes, cooking takes about 40 minutes.

Pasta with Basil & Tomato Sauce

Use fully ripened tomatoes for this recipe, otherwise the sauce will be bland.

SERVES 4

1 pound pasta
3 Tbsps olive oil
1 clove garlic, chopped
3 tomatoes, skinned, seeded, and chopped
Salt and freshly ground black pepper
10 fresh basil leaves, finely chopped

Cook the pasta in plenty of boiling, salted water for 10-12 minutes, or until *al dente*. Rinse under hot water and set aside to drain.

Heat the olive oil in a skillet, add the garlic, tomatoes, and some salt and pepper and fry gently for about 12 minutes, stirring frequently. Stir the drained pasta into the sauce, mix well, and heat through. Stir in the basil and check the seasoning just before serving.

Time: Preparation takes 5 minutes, cooking takes 15 minutes.

Fettuccini with Garlic & Oil

Serve this simple recipe as a supper dish with a salad or use it to accompany a casserole.

SERVES 2

10 ounces green fettuccini
⅔ cup olive oil
3 garlic cloves, finely chopped
2 Tbsps chopped fresh parsley
Salt and freshly ground black pepper

Cook the fettuccini in plenty of boiling, salted water for 10-12 minutes, or until *al dente*.

Meanwhile, heat the oil in a skillet and, when warm, add the garlic. Fry gently until golden-brown, then add the chopped parsley and some salt and pepper to taste.

Drain the pasta and transfer to a hot serving dish. Add the sauce and toss to coat the pasta well. Serve hot.

Time: Preparation takes 5 minutes, cooking takes 10 minutes.

Cook's Tip: Use extra-virgin olive oil for this recipe as it has a superior flavor.

Spaghetti with Pesto

Pesto is a very versatile sauce – it can be stirred into pasta, soups or any number of sauces.

SERVES 4

5 Tbsps olive oil

2 garlic cloves, finely chopped

2 Tbsps pine nuts

1 cup fresh basil leaves

3 Tbsps grated Parmesan or pecorino cheese

Salt and freshly ground black pepper

10 ounces spaghetti

Fresh basil to garnish

Heat 1 tablespoon of the oil over a low heat, add the garlic and pine nuts, and cook until the pine nuts are a light golden-brown. Grind the basil leaves, pine nuts, and garlic in a blender or food processor. When smooth, add the remaining oil in a thin, steady stream, blending continuously. Place the mixture in a bowl and stir in the cheese, adding salt and pepper to taste.

Meanwhile, cook the spaghetti in a large pan of boiling, salted water for 10-12 minutes, or until *al dente*. Drain well and toss the pesto through the pasta. Serve with a side-dish of extra grated cheese, and garnish with fresh basil.

Time: Preparation takes 15 minutes, cooking takes 15 minutes.

Seafood Chow Mein

Chow Mein is a wonderful combination of noodles and vegetables in a rich sauce or gravy. The addition of clams and mussels, or other seafood, makes it extra special.

SERVES 4

8 ounces Chinese egg noodles

½ green bell pepper

½ red bell pepper

1 Tbsp oil

1 garlic clove, chopped

½ tsp chopped fresh root ginger

½ green onion (scallion), chopped

¼ cup cooked, shelled mussels

¼ cup cooked shelled clams

1 Tbsp Chinese wine

2 Tbsps soy sauce

Salt and freshly ground black pepper

Cook the noodles in boiling, salted water until just tender, then rinse under cold water and set aside to drain.

Cut the peppers into thin slices. Heat the oil in a wok and stir-fry the garlic, ginger, peppers, and scallion for 1 minute. Stir in the mussels and clams, the Chinese wine, soy sauce, and the cooked noodles. Mix together well and season with salt and pepper to taste. Serve when heated through completely.

Time: Preparation takes 15 minutes, cooking takes 15 minutes.

Cook's Tip: Mix the noodles carefully through the sauce to heat without breaking them up.

Spaghetti with Sorrel & -Cheese Sauce-

Sorrel is very similar to spinach. In this recipe it produces a delicious and unusual dish.

SERVES 4

1 pound spaghetti

1 cup sorrel leaves

1¼ cups chicken or vegetable broth

1 Tbsp butter or margarine

1 Tbsp all-purpose flour

½ cup heavy cream

4 Tbsps grated Pecorino cheese

Salt and freshly ground black pepper

Pinch of cayenne pepper

2 hard-cooked eggs, roughly chopped

Grated Parmesan cheese

Cook the spaghetti in a large pan of boiling, salted water for 10-12 minutes, or until *al dente*. Discard any thick stems from the sorrel, then cook the leaves in the broth for 4 minutes.

Melt the butter in a separate saucepan, stir in the flour, and heat for 1 minute. Purée the sorrel and broth in a blender or food processor and gradually add to the butter-and-flour roux, stirring constantly. Bring to a boil, stirring continuously.

Once the sauce has thickened, stir in the cream, cheese, salt and pepper, and cayenne pepper, and carefully stir in the eggs. Heat the sauce gently, pour it over the drained pasta, and add grated Parmesan cheese before serving.

Time: Preparation takes 10 minutes, cooking takes about 15 minutes.

Nutty Spaghetti

Peanut butter and lemon juice give a lovely flavor to this delicious vegetarian dish.

SERVES

8 ounces spaghetti

1 onion, finely chopped

2 Tbsps sunflower oil

2½ tsps curry powder

¼ cup tomato juice

3 Tbsps crunchy peanut butter

1 Tbsp lemon juice

Lemon twists and peanuts to garnish

Cook the spaghetti in plenty of boiling, salted water for 10-12 minutes, or until *al dente*, then drain well.

Fry the onion in the oil until golden-brown, then stir in the curry powder, tomato juice, peanut butter, and lemon juice. Simmer for 5 minutes and then stir the sauce into the spaghetti. Garnish with lemon twists and peanuts before serving.

Time: Preparation takes 5 minutes, cooking takes about 15 minutes.

Variation: Almond butter and blanched almonds can be used in place of the peanut butter and peanuts.

Spaghetti à la Genovese

The use of less basil and addition of parsley makes this sauce slightly less expensive than the very similar pesto sauce.

SERVES 4

2 Tbsps fresh basil leaves

1 Tbsp fresh parsley

1 clove garlic, finely chopped

4 Tbsps pine nuts or chopped walnuts

4 Tbsps grated Parmesan cheese

Salt and freshly ground black pepper

⅔ cup olive oil

1 pound spaghetti

Combine the basil, parsley, garlic, nuts, cheese, and some salt and pepper in a food processor or blender. Process until finely chopped. With the machine running, pour the oil in through the funnel in a thin, steady stream. Process until smooth and thick, with the consistency of mayonnaise.

Cook the spaghetti in a large pan of boiling, salted water for 10-12 minutes, or until *al dente*. Drain the pasta, rinse well in boiling water, and drain again. Pour the sauce over the pasta in a serving dish and toss together well to serve. Serve with additional grated cheese if wished.

Time: Preparation takes 15 minutes, cooking takes 15 minutes.

Fried Noodles, Pork & Vegetables

Ensure the boiled noodles are well dried before frying to prevent any spatter.

SERVES 4

12 ounces fresh Chinese egg noodles
1 taro root
1 Tbsp oil
1 clove garlic, chopped
1 carrot, cut into sticks
½ head Chinese (Napa) cabbage, shredded
8 ounces cooked pork, thinly sliced
1 Tbsp soy sauce
1¼ cups chicken broth
Salt and freshly ground black pepper
Oil for deep-frying
1 tsp cornstarch, combined with a little water

Cook the noodles in boiling, salted water until just tender. Rinse in warm water and set aside to drain. Slice the end off the taro, peel with a potato peeler, and cut into thin slices.

Heat the oil in a wok and stir-fry the taro, garlic, carrot, and Chinese (Napa) cabbage. Add the pork, soy sauce, broth, and salt and pepper. Cook over a gentle heat for 5 minutes, shaking the wok frequently.

Heat the oil for deep-frying to 350 degrees and fry the noodles a few at a time. Drain the noodles on absorbent kitchen paper. Divide the noodles equally between four small plates.

Remove the vegetable-and-pork mixture from the wok with a slotted spoon and serve over the noodles. Stir the cornstarch mixture into the remaining sauce in the wok and stir until the sauce boils and thickens. Pour some over each plate of noodles and serve immediately.

Time: Preparation takes 10 minutes, cooking takes about 20 minutes.

Pasta with Leeks & — Mussels —

Mussels and leeks combine well in this tasty dinner entrée.

SERVES 6

2 cups mussels in the shell
½ cup white wine
1 shallot, chopped
2 medium leeks
¾ cup heavy cream
Salt and freshly ground black pepper
1 pound pasta spirals
2 slices ham
2 Tbsps butter
Chopped fresh chives to garnish

Scrub the mussels, remove the beards, and wash in several changes of water to remove any sand. Discard any open shells which do not shut when lightly tapped. Place the mussels, white wine, and the chopped shallot in a large saucepan. Cover the pan and cook over a high heat for about 5 minutes, or just until the mussels open. Cool, and remove the mussels from their shells. Discard any that have not opened. Reserve the cooking liquid.

Quarter each leek lengthwise, wash thoroughly under running water, and slice finely. Put the leeks and cream, with salt and pepper to taste, in a saucepan. Cover and cook over a low heat for 10 minutes. Add the pasta to a large pan of boiling, salted water and cook for 10-12 minutes, or until *al dente*. Stir the pasta occasionally to prevent it from sticking. Drain, and rinse well in cold water. Remove any fat or rind from the ham before slicing it into small pieces.

Strain the mussel liquor through a strainer lined with cheesecloth. Measure out about ⅔ cup. Add the shelled mussels and the measured mussel liquor to the cream mixture and cook for 4 minutes, stirring constantly. Melt the butter in a sauté pan, add the pasta, and reheat gently with the ham. Season to taste. When the pasta is heated through, add the creamy mussel-and-leek sauce. Serve garnished with some chopped chives.

Time: Preparation takes 30 minutes, cooking takes 25 minutes.

Cook's Tip: Use a good quality ham to ensure a lovely flavor and texture.

Spirali with Spinach & Bacon

A quick and tasty dish to prepare – add a little freshly grated nutmeg if wished; it is the perfect partner for spinach.

SERVES 4

12 ounces pasta spirals

2 cups raw spinach

3 slices lean bacon

1 small red or green chili

1 small red bell pepper

1 small onion

3 Tbsps olive oil

1 clove garlic, finely chopped

Salt and freshly ground black pepper

Cook the pasta in boiling, salted water for 10-12 minutes, or until *al dente*. Drain in a colander and rinse under hot water. Keep the pasta in a bowl of hot water until ready to use.

Tear the stalks off the spinach and wash the leaves well. Set aside to drain. Remove any rind from the bacon and dice the bacon finely. Cut the chili and the red bell pepper in half, discard the seeds, and slice the flesh finely. Slice the onion thinly. Roll up several of the spinach leaves into a cigar shape and shred finely. Repeat until all the spinach is shredded.

Heat the oil in a sauté pan or skillet and add the garlic, onion, chili pepper, and bacon. Fry for 2 minutes then add the spinach and fry for 2 minutes more, stirring continuously. Season with salt and pepper. Drain the pasta and toss in a colander to remove excess water. Mix with the spinach sauce and serve immediately.

Time: Preparation takes about 15 minutes, cooking takes 15 minutes.

Cook's Tip: Wash the spinach leaves in cold water to keep them crisp.

Smoked Fish with Peas & Pasta

Smoked fish combines very well with pasta.

SERVES 4

1¼ cups milk

2 medium smoked fish fillets (trout or whitefish)

2 Tbsps butter or margarine

2 Tbsps all-purpose flour

1 Tbsp chopped fresh chives

1 Tbsp chopped fresh parsley

3 Tbsps cooked peas

1 hard-cooked egg, chopped

Salt and freshly ground black pepper

8 ounces pasta shells, cooked

Heat the milk gently in a large sauté pan with a tight-fitting lid. Add the fish when the milk is warm, cover the pan, and poach the fish gently for about 8 minutes. Check the pan occasionally, adding a little more milk if necessary. When cooked, drain the fish, reserving the milk.

Melt the butter in a saucepan, stir in the flour and heat gently for a few minutes. Add the reserved milk, stirring continuously. Heat until the sauce boils and thickens; if it is too thick, add a little more milk. Add the chives and parsley to the sauce and pour it into a large bowl.

Flake the fish, removing any bones. Add the fish to the sauce, along with the peas, hard-cooked egg, and salt and pepper. Stir well, then add the drained pasta to the sauce, and mix gently to distribute the fish evenly. Return the mixture to a large saucepan and heat gently for 3-4 minutes. Serve immediately.

Time: Preparation takes 10 minutes, cooking takes 25 minutes.

Serving Idea: Serve with a tossed green salad.

Lasagne Rolls

This quick and easy dish is perfect for a mid-week supper.

SERVES 4

2 tsps vegetable oil
8 sheets lasagne
¼ cup button mushrooms
1 small boneless chicken breast
3 Tbsps butter or margarine
2 Tbsps all-purpose flour
⅔ cup milk
1 cup grated Swiss or Cheddar cheese
Salt and freshly ground black pepper

Fill a large saucepan two-thirds full with salted water. Add the oil and bring to a boil. Add 1 sheet of lasagne, wait about 2 minutes, then add another sheet. Cook only a few at a time and when *al dente*, after about 6-7 minutes, remove from the boiling water and rinse under cold water. Allow to drain on a kitchen towel. Repeat this process until all the lasagne is cooked.

Slice the mushrooms. Cut the chicken breast into thin strips across the grain. Melt half the butter in a small skillet and fry the mushrooms and the chicken for about 10 minutes, until the chicken is just cooked. In a small saucepan, melt the remaining butter. Stir in the flour and heat gently for 1 minute. Remove the pan from the heat and gradually add the milk, stirring well. Return the pan to the heat and bring to a boil, stirring constantly. Cook for 3 minutes. Pour the sauce over the chicken and mushrooms. Add half the cheese, mix well and season to taste.

Lay the sheets of lasagne on a board and divide the chicken mixture equally between them. Spread the chicken mixture over each lasagne sheet and roll up lengthwise, like a jellyroll or burrito. Place the rolls in an ovenproof dish. Sprinkle with the remaining cheese and broil under a preheated moderate broiler, until the cheese is bubbly and golden-brown.

Time: Preparation takes 10 minutes, cooking takes 15 minutes.

Variation: For a delicious vegetarian alternative, use blue cheese and broccoli flowerets instead of the chicken breasts.

Mee Goreng

This Indonesian dish of noodles is quick to prepare, but be sure you have everything chopped before you start cooking.

SERVES 4

8 ounces fine Chinese egg noodles
4 Tbsps peanut oil
1 onion, finely chopped
2 garlic cloves, finely chopped
1 green chili, seeded and finely sliced
1 tsp chili paste or chili sauce
4 ounces pork fillet, finely sliced crosswise
2 sticks of celery, sliced
¼ small white cabbage, finely shredded
Salt and freshly ground black pepper
1 Tbsp light soy sauce
4 cooked peeled shrimp

Soak the noodles in hot water, until they are soft. Rinse in cold water and drain thoroughly in a colander.

Heat the oil in a wok and stir-fry the onion, garlic, and chili until the onion is soft and just golden-brown. Add the chili paste, stir well, then add the pork, celery, and cabbage to the fried onions. Stir-fry for about 3 minutes, or until the pork is cooked through. Season to taste. Stir in the soy sauce, drained noodles, and shrimp. Toss the mixture together and heat through before serving.

Time: Preparation takes 20 minutes, cooking takes 15 minutes.

Serving Idea: Serve with plain boiled rice and shrimp crackers.

Shanghai Noodles

Noodles are more popular in the north of China than in the rice-growing areas of the south. In Shanghai, both are popular.

SERVES 4

3 Tbsps oil
1 small chicken breast, thinly sliced
1 pound thick Shanghai noodles or fettuccini
½ head Chinese (Napa) cabbage, shredded
4 green onions (scallions), thinly sliced
2 Tbsps soy sauce
Freshly ground black pepper
Dash of sesame oil

Heat the oil in a wok, add the chicken, and stir-fry for 2-3 minutes.

Meanwhile, cook the noodles in boiling, salted water until just tender. Drain well in a colander and rinse under hot water. Toss in the colander to drain again and leave to dry.

Add the shredded Chinese (Napa) cabbage and green onions (scallions) to the chicken in the wok, along with the soy sauce, pepper and sesame oil. Cook for about 1 minute then toss in the cooked noodles. Stir well and heat through. Serve immediately.

Time: Preparation takes 10 minutes, cooking takes 6-8 minutes.

Variation: Pork may be substituted for the chicken. Add shredded fresh spinach with the Chinese (Napa) cabbage.

Penne with Anchovy Sauce

This is an unusual sauce but one which makes good use of that favorite Italian ingredient, the anchovy.

SERVES 4

6-8 canned anchovy fillets, drained

2 Tbsps olive oil

14-ounce can chopped tomatoes

3 Tbsps chopped fresh parsley

Freshly ground black pepper

10 ounces penne

2 Tbsps melted butter or margarine

2 Tbsps grated Parmesan cheese

Chop the anchovies and cook them briefly in the oil, stirring until they break up into a paste. Add the chopped tomatoes with the parsley, and black pepper to taste. Bring to a boil, then reduce the heat and simmer, uncovered, for 10 minutes.

Meanwhile, cook the penne in plenty of boiling salted water for 10-12 minutes, or until *al dente*. Rinse in hot water and drain well. Toss the penne in the melted butter. Combine the sauce with the pasta, sprinkle with a little extra chopped parsley, and serve immediately with grated Parmesan cheese.

Time: Preparation takes 15 minutes, cooking takes 20 minutes.

Pasta Spirals & Creamy Parsley Sauce

This light supper dish is delicious by itself or with chicken or fish.

SERVES 4

2 Tbsps butter or margarine

1 Tbsp all-purpose flour

1¼ cups milk

10 ounces pasta spirals

1 Tbsp lemon juice, or 2 tsps wine vinegar

1 Tbsp chopped fresh parsley

Salt and freshly ground black pepper

Melt the butter in a saucepan, then stir in flour. Cook for 1 minute. Remove the pan from the heat and gradually stir in the milk. Return to the heat and stir constantly until boiling. Cook for 2 minutes.

Meanwhile, cook the pasta spirals in plenty of boiling, salted water for 10-12 minutes, or until *al dente*. Rinse in hot water and drain well. Add the lemon juice and parsley to the sauce and stir well. Season if necessary. Pour the sauce over the pasta and mix well. Serve immediately.

Time: Preparation takes 5 minutes, cooking takes 15 minutes.

Variation: Use tricolored pasta spirals for a more colorful dish.

Entrées

Pasta entrées can be cooked in a variety of ways, besides boiling. Apart from lasagne and some cannelloni, which do not need cooking before baking, all wheat-based pasta needs to be parboiled before being baked or fried. Pasta for baking should be boiled until just *al dente*, then rinsed in cold water to prevent sticking.

This section contains recipes for a wide variety of pasta types, cooked in as many different ways as possible, to give you plenty of ideas for serving pasta as an entrée. We have also tried to vary the ingredients and sauces as far as possible. Of course, you can always think up substitutes for the vegetables, meats, fish, and seafood suggestions.

Hearty baked pasta dishes are popular in many countries. They include Pastitsio (page 65) from the eastern Mediterranean and several cannelloni dishes such as Cannelloni (page 77) and Tuna Cannelloni (page 70). These baked dishes are known as "rib-stickers," filling foods to keep you warm in the icy blasts of a European winter. Spicy Steamed Pork with Noodles (page 63), on the other hand, has a tang of the Orient about it, as does Chinese Chicken with Pasta (page 64).

For those who prefer meat-free meals there are a number of delicious options, including Zucchini and Nut Lasagne with Eggplants (page 62). If company are coming, they will enjoy Spaghetti with Crab and Bacon (page 66). And how about showing what you can do by making your own pasta and serving it as Salmon and Fennel Lasagne (page 69).

Flavored pasta makes an exciting entrée. Try soba, Japanese buckwheat noodles, instead of macaroni, or any of the whole-wheat varieties of pasta which are becoming more and more popular. Whole-wheat pasta is also the healthier option, of course. Herbed pasta, especially if it homemade, makes a particularly good side-dish with dairy foods or meats.

Pasta entrées are quick to prepare, filling, and very acceptable, so they are the perfect solution to the problem of what to feed to an unexpected guest. But they are just as useful as an everyday stand-by and are enjoyed by the whole family.

Zucchini & Nut Lasagne with Eggplants

Not all lasagnes are made with a meat sauce – this delicious variation is light and fragrant and is the perfect vegetarian dinner party dish.

SERVES 4-6

12 sheets of whole-wheat lasagne

6 Tbsps pine nuts

2 Tbsps butter

3 cups trimmed and sliced zucchini

1¼ cups ricotta cheese

½ tsp grated nutmeg

1 Tbsp olive oil

1 large eggplant, sliced

⅔ cup water

Salt and freshly ground black pepper

6 Tbsps grated cheddar cheese

Cook the lasagne in plenty of boiling, salted water for 8-10 minutes, then drain and spread out on kitchen towels until required.

Place the pine nuts in a dry skillet and toast gently over a low heat, tossing the pan frequently for 2 minutes, or until lightly browned. Set to one side. Melt the butter in the pan and cook the zucchini, adding a little water if necessary, until just tender. Combine the zucchini and pine nuts with the ricotta cheese, then add the nutmeg and mix thoroughly.

Heat the olive oil in a separate skillet and cook the eggplant slices for 4 minutes. Add the water and simmer, covered, until soft. Season with salt and pepper. Blend in a blender or food processor until smooth, adding a little extra water if necessary.

Place 4 sheets of lasagne in the bottom of a greased, ovenproof dish and top with half the zucchini mixture. Place another 4 sheets of lasagne over the zucchini and add half the eggplant sauce, followed by the remaining zucchini. Cover with the rest of the lasagne and the remaining sauce. Top with the grated cheese and bake in an oven preheated to 375 degrees for 40 minutes, or until the cheese is golden-brown.

Time: Preparation takes 30 minutes, cooking takes 50 minutes.

Serving Idea: Serve with jacket potatoes and a green salad.

Spaghetti Bolognese

This must surely be one of the great classic dishes of the world.

SERVES 4

2 Tbsps butter or margarine

1 Tbsp olive oil

2 onions, finely chopped

1 carrot, diced

1 cup ground beef

½ cup tomato paste

Salt and freshly ground black pepper

1¼ cups beef broth

2 Tbsps sherry

10 ounces spaghetti

Grated Parmesan cheese

Heat the butter and oil in a pan and cook the onions and carrot slowly until soft. Increase the heat and add the ground beef. Fry for a few minutes, then stir, and continue cooking until the meat is browned all over. Add the tomato paste, salt, and pepper and the broth. Simmer gently for about 45 minutes, stirring occasionally, until the mixture thickens. Add the sherry to the sauce and cook for a further 5 minutes.

Meanwhile, cook the spaghetti in a large pan of boiling salted water, for 10-12 minutes, or until *al dente*. Drain well and divide the spaghetti among heated serving plates. Top with the Bolognese sauce and accompany with some grated Parmesan.

Time: Preparation takes 10 minutes, cooking takes 1 hour 15 minutes.

Spicy Steamed Pork -with Noodles-

The combination of spicy meatballs, bok choy, noodles, and fresh coriander (cilantro) makes a simple but memorable dish.

SERVES 4

1 cup lean ground pork

1 tsp ground coriander (cilantro)

1 tsp ground cumin

1 tsp ground turmeric

1 bunch bok choy or spinach, washed

1-2 Tbsps red or green curry paste

1 tsp shrimp paste

⅔ cup thick coconut milk

6 ounces egg noodles

Chopped fresh coriander (cilantro), to garnish

Place the ground pork and ground spices in a food processor and process until smooth. Shape the pork mixture into small balls using dampened hands.

Tear the bok choy into large pieces and place in a heatproof dish that will fit into a steamer. Arrange the meatballs on top. Mix together the curry paste, shrimp paste, and coconut milk, and pour over the meatballs. Cover and steam for 20 minutes.

Meanwhile, cook the noodles in a large pan of boiling, salted water until tender. Drain well, then mix the noodles together with the pork and bok choy. Garnish with a sprinkling of chopped coriander (cilantro) leaves.

Time: Preparation takes 20 minutes, cooking takes 20 minutes.

Variation: The pork and spices can be mixed by hand. Add a little beaten egg, if necessary, to bind the mixture together.

Lasagne with Four Cheeses

This is a well-flavored, mixed cheese lasagne, suitable for vegetarians.

SERVES 4

8 ounces green lasagne
4 Tbsps butter
3 Tbsps all-purpose flour
2¼ cups milk
3 Tbsps grated Parmesan cheese
2 Tbsps grated Gruyère cheese
¼ cup diced Mozzarella
¼ cup diced Pecorino
Salt and freshly ground black pepper and nutmeg

Cook the lasagne a few sheets at a time, in plenty of boiling, salted water. Plunge the cooked pasta into cold water then spread out on clean paper towels.

Melt the butter in a pan, add the flour, and stir over a low heat for 1 minute. Remove the pan from the heat and gradually add the milk, stirring well. Bring to a boil, stirring continuously, then add all the cheeses (except 2 tablespoonfuls of the Parmesan) and salt, pepper and nutmeg to taste. Stir until the cheeses have melted.

Butter an ovenproof dish and place a layer of lasagne in the bottom. Top with some of the sauce, then continue layering, finishing with a layer of sauce. Top with the reserved Parmesan cheese and bake in an oven preheated to 350 degrees for about 45 minutes, until well browned. Serve with a green salad.
Time: Preparation takes 10 minutes, cooking takes 1 hour.

Chinese Chicken with Pasta

This is not a classic Chinese dish, but it is delicious all the same!

SERVES 2

2 boneless chicken breasts, skinned
Grated rind and juice of ½ lime
Small piece fresh root ginger, peeled and finely grated
1 clove garlic, finely chopped
1 Tbsp sesame oil
2 Tbsps light soy sauce
6 ounces fettuccini
2 Tbsps butter
Salt and freshly ground black pepper
Chopped fresh parsley to garnish

Place the chicken breasts in a small ovenproof dish. Mix together the lime rind and juice, the ginger, garlic, sesame oil, and soy sauce, and pour this over the chicken. Leave in a cool place to marinate for 4 hours.

Bake the chicken in the marinade in an oven preheated to 375 degrees, for 30 minutes, turning once. Increase the heat to 425 degrees for the last 5 minutes of cooking time.

Meanwhile, cook the pasta in plenty of boiling, salted water for 10-12 minutes or until *al dente*. Drain, then rinse in boiling water and drain again.

Melt the butter in the pasta pan, add the fettuccini and some black pepper, and toss until mixed. Slice the chicken and add to the pasta with any remaining sauce. Add extra butter if necessary and serve immediately, topped with some chopped parsley.
Time: Preparation takes 15 minutes, plus marinating time. Cooking takes 30 minutes.

Pastitsio

This baked macaroni dish is eaten in Malta, Greece and Cyprus.

SERVES 4

8 ounces macaroni
⅓ cup butter or margarine
4 Tbsps grated Parmesan cheese
Pinch of grated nutmeg
Salt and freshly ground black pepper
2 eggs, beaten
1 medium onion, chopped
1 clove garlic, finely chopped
2 cups ground beef
2 Tbsps tomato paste
⅓ cup beef broth
2 Tbsps chopped fresh parsley
4 Tbsps red wine
2 Tbsps all-purpose flour
1¼ cups milk

Cook the macaroni in plenty of boiling, salted water for 10-12 minutes, or until *al dente*. Rinse under hot water and drain. Place one-third of the butter in the saucepan and return the macaroni to it. Add half the cheese, the nutmeg, and salt and pepper to taste. Leave to cool slightly then mix in half the beaten egg and set aside.

Melt half of the remaining butter in a skillet and fry the onion and garlic gently until the onion is soft. Increase the heat, add the meat, and fry until browned.

Add the tomato paste, broth, parsley, and wine, and season with salt and pepper. Simmer for 20 minutes.

In a small pan, melt the rest of the butter, stir in the flour, and cook for 30 seconds. Remove from the heat and stir in the milk. Return to the heat and bring to a boil, stirring constantly, until the sauce thickens. Beat in the remaining egg and season to taste.

Spoon half the macaroni into a serving dish and cover with the meat sauce. Add another layer of macaroni. Pour the white sauce over the top and sprinkle with the remaining cheese. Bake in an oven preheated to 375 degrees for 30 minutes or until golden-brown on top. Serve immediately.

Time: Preparation takes 10 minutes, cooking takes 1 hour.
Serving Idea: Serve with green vegetables and crusty bread.

Spaghetti with Crab & Bacon

Bacon and crab combine well to make a really flavorsome and luxurious dish.

SERVES 4

1 bunch fresh parsley

4 cups all-purpose flour

4 eggs, lightly beaten

8-ounce slab lean bacon

3 Tbsps butter

1½ cups crabmeat

1¼ cups heavy cream

1 Tbsp olive oil

Salt and freshly ground black pepper

Chopped fresh chervil

Trim the leaves off the parsley. Cook the parsley for 10 minutes in boiling water then press through a fine strainer. Reserve the cooking liquid. Purée the parsley with 3 tablespoons of the cooking liquid in a blender or food processor.

Place the flour in a bowl and make a well in the center. Add the eggs and 1½ tablespoons of the parsley purée then mix together to form a dough. Knead lightly on a board then form into a ball. Divide the dough into four and form these pieces into balls. Press each ball flat and run it through a pasta machine until thinly rolled, or roll out by hand with a rolling pin. Pass through the spaghetti cutter, or cut finely with a sharp knife. Spread the spaghetti out on a clean cloth to dry for a few minutes.

Cut the rind off the bacon and cut the meat into small dice. Heat the butter in a large skillet or saucepan and when it bubbles, add the bacon and cook for 3-4 minutes. Shred the crabmeat then add it to the cream and heat gently in a saucepan.

Meanwhile, add the olive oil to a large pan of boiling, salted water and cook the spaghetti for 5 minutes, or until *al dente*. Drain and rinse in hot water. Add the drained spaghetti to the bacon, mix well, and season with salt and pepper. Place the hot buttered spaghetti around the edge of a serving dish and pour the crab mixture into the center. Garnish with the chervil.

Time: Preparation takes 1 hour, cooking takes 20 minutes.

Variation: Use crabsticks instead of fresh crabmeat.

Brasciole with Fettuccini

This elegant dish is perfect for a dinner party. The veal rolls may be prepared in advance and refrigerated until needed.

SERVES 4

4 veal steaks

4 thin slices ham

2 Tbsps grated Parmesan cheese

Salt and freshly ground black pepper

2 Tbsps butter or margarine

14-ounce can tomatoes, sieved, or 2 cups tomato sauce

8 ounces fettuccini

Bat the veal steaks out thinly between two sheets of dampened parchment paper. Place a slice of ham on top of each steak and sprinkle each with 1 tablespoon of the Parmesan cheese and some salt and freshly ground black pepper. Roll up from a short side, like a jellyroll or burrito, tucking the sides in to form neat parcels. Tie gently with string at each end and in the middle.

Heat the butter in a pan and add the veal rolls. Cook gently until lightly browned all over. Add the sieved tomatoes, cover, and cook for 15 minutes.

Meanwhile, cook the fettuccini in plenty of boiling, salted water for 10-12 minutes, or until *al dente*. Rinse in hot water and drain.

Remove the string and cut the veal rolls into 1-inch slices. Toss the fettuccini together with the tomato sauce and top with the veal and remaining grated Parmesan cheese. Serve immediately.

Time: Preparation takes 15 minutes, cooking takes 25 minutes.

Penne with Spicy Chili Sauce

Penne are thicker than macaroni so more sauce gets trapped inside the tubes.

SERVES 4-6

1 Tbsp olive oil

2 garlic cloves, finely chopped

1 onion, chopped

4 slices bacon, rind removed, chopped

14-ounce can chopped plum tomatoes

2 red chilies, seeded and chopped

2 green onions (scallions), chopped

4 Tbsps grated Pecorino or Parmesan cheese

1 pound penne or macaroni

Salt and freshly ground black pepper

Heat the oil in a skillet and fry the garlic, onion, and bacon gently for 6-8 minutes. Add the tomatoes, chilies, green onions (scallions) and half the cheese. Simmer gently for 20 minutes then season to taste.

Cook the penne or macaroni in a large pan of boiling, salted water for 10-12 minutes, or until *al dente*. Rinse under hot water and drain well.

Place the cooked penne in a warmed serving dish with half the sauce and toss them together to coat the pasta. Pour the remaining sauce over the top and sprinkle with the remaining cheese before serving.

Time: Preparation takes 15 minutes, cooking takes about 30 minutes.

Variation: For a vegetarian meal substitute ½ cup mushrooms for the bacon.

Spaghetti with Sweetbread —Carbonara—

Sweetbreads are used in place of bacon for this variation of a popular classic.

SERVES 4

12 ounces whole-wheat spaghetti

1 onion, chopped

3 Tbsps olive oil

8 ounces calves' sweetbreads, blanched, skinned, and chopped

⅓ cup dry white wine

4 eggs, lightly beaten

4 Tbsps grated Parmesan cheese

2 Tbsps freshly chopped basil

1 clove garlic, finely chopped

Salt and freshly ground black pepper

Fresh basil, to garnish

Cook the spaghetti in a large pan of boiling, salted water for about 10-12 minutes, or until *al dente*.

Meanwhile, fry the onion gently in the olive oil for 5 minutes. Add the chopped sweetbreads to the pan and fry gently for 4 minutes, then add the white wine and cook briskly until it has almost evaporated. Beat the eggs with the Parmesan cheese, basil, garlic and some salt and pepper.

Drain the pasta thoroughly; immediately stir in the beaten egg mixture and the sweetbreads, so that the heat from the spaghetti cooks the eggs. Garnish with some basil leaves and serve immediately.

Time: Preparation takes 10 minutes, cooking takes about 12 minutes.

Salmon & Fennel Lasagne

Salmon and fennel make a luxurious lasagne for a special occasion.

SERVES 4

Pasta dough
3 cups all-purpose flour

3 eggs, beaten

Filling
2 Tbsps butter

1 Tbsp all-purpose flour

1¼ cups milk

1¼ pounds fresh salmon (in one piece if possible)

1 tsp fennel seeds

Salt and freshly ground black pepper

1 cup fish broth

3 Tbsps grated Swiss cheese

P lace the flour in a mixing bowl and make a well in the center. Add the eggs and work to a dough. On a board, knead well until smooth and set aside to rest for 30 minutes.

Roll the dough out very thinly into long strips, using a pasta machine or rolling pin. Cut into rectangles. Parboil the pasta in boiling, salted water for 1 minute. Drain and then spread out on dampened kitchen towels, without overlapping the strips.

To prepare the filling, melt the butter in a saucepan and stir in the flour. Cook gently for 1 minute. Remove from the heat and gradually add the milk. Return the pan to the heat and bring the sauce to a boil, stirring continuously. Cook for 3 minutes.

Cut the salmon into long, thin slices, similar to lox (smoked salmon) slices. Remove all the bones. Butter an ovenproof dish and place some strips of pasta in it. Build up layers of white sauce, a few fennel seeds, the salmon, salt and pepper, and then another layer of pasta. Continue layering, finishing with a layer of pasta. Add the broth and then top with the cheese. Bake in an oven preheated to 375 degrees for 20-25 minutes, or until the broth has been almost completely absorbed. Serve hot.

Time: Preparation takes 40 minutes, cooking takes about 35 minutes.

Cook's Tip: This lasagne should be slightly crisp on top. If necessary, place the dish under the broiler for 1 minute before serving.

Tuna Cannelloni

Cannelloni are easy to prepare but rinse the tubes well after boiling, to prevent them from sticking together.

SERVES 4

12 cannelloni shells

Filling

2 Tbsps butter or margarine

1 onion, chopped

⅔ cup mushrooms, chopped

1 stick celery, chopped

1 Tbsp all-purpose flour

⅔ cup milk

4 Tbsps heavy cream

4 Tbsps mayonnaise

1 Tbsp chopped fresh oregano

1 cup canned tuna, undrained

Salt and freshly ground black pepper

3 shallots, chopped

1 egg, lightly beaten

Topping

4 Tbsps fresh bread crumbs

4 Tbsps grated cheese

1 Tbsp butter or margarine

Cook the cannelloni shells in a large pan of boiling, salted water for 15-20 minutes, or until *al dente*. Rinse in hot water and drain well.

Meanwhile, melt the butter for the filling in a saucepan. Add the onion and cook until transparent, then add the mushrooms and celery and cook for 5 minutes. Stir in the flour and cook until light golden-brown. Gradually add the milk, stirring continuously. Bring to a boil and cook for 3 minutes, stirring all the time. Add the cream, mayonnaise, oregano, and the undrained, flaked tuna. Season with salt and pepper and stir until boiling, then simmer for 3 minutes. Add the shallots and egg, and mix in well.

Spoon the mixture into the cannelloni shells and place in an ovenproof dish. Mix the bread crumbs and cheese together and scatter this over the cannelloni, then dot with butter or margarine. Bake for 20 minutes in an oven preheated to 375 degrees. Serve immediately.

Time: Preparation takes 15 minutes, cooking takes 45 minutes.

Lasagne with Seafood

This seafood lasagne does not have a sauce topping, so it is covered with foil during baking to prevent it from drying out.

SERVES 4-6

4 cups all-purpose flour

4 eggs, lightly beaten

2 cups raw clams

3 cups raw mussels

2 cups raw shrimp

1 cup dry white wine

2 shallots, chopped

1 onion, finely chopped

2 garlic cloves, finely chopped

4 Tbsps olive oil

6 tomatoes, skinned, seeded, and crushed

2 Tbsps chopped fresh parsley

Salt and freshly ground black pepper

3 Tbsps melted butter

4 Tbsps grated Gruyère cheese

2 tsps chopped fresh chervil

Place the flour in a mixing bowl and make a well in the center. Add the eggs and mix together, using a fork and then your fingers to form a dough. Shape into a ball and knead until smooth. Wrap the dough in plastic wrap and leave to rest in a cool place for 15 minutes.

Divide the dough into 4 and flatten each piece before passing it through the rollers of a pasta machine. Continue rolling until long, thin strips of pasta are formed. Flour the rollers as necessary during the process. Alternatively, use a rolling pin. Cut the pasta into rectangles and leave to dry on clean kitchen towels for about 30 minutes.

Wash and scrub the clams and mussels, and rinse well. Discard any with broken shells or any open ones that will not shut when lightly tapped. Peel the shrimp and cut in half lengthwise if they are very large. Pour the wine into a flameproof casserole, add the shallots and clams and cook, covered, over a high heat for 3-4 minutes or until they open. Remove the clams with a slotted spoon, then add the mussels to the same liquid and cook for about 5 minutes or until they open. Remove the clams and mussels from their shells, discarding any that have not opened. Fry the onions and garlic in 2 tablespoons of the olive oil in a skillet. Add the tomatoes and half the chopped parsley. Strain the broth through a strainer lined with cheesecloth. Add to the pan with the shrimp and cook over a moderate heat for 15-20 minutes. Season to taste, add the clams and mussels, and remove from the heat.

While the sauce is cooking, bring a large pan of salted water to a boil. Add the rest of the olive oil and cook the lasagne, a few sheets at a time, for 3 minutes. Refresh the lasagne under cold water, then spread out on the kitchen towels until required.

Brush an ovenproof baking dish with some of the butter. Layer the sheets of lasagne with the seafood mixture. Brush the pasta with butter each time. Finish with a layer of lasagne and brush it with butter. Top with the cheese and remaining parsley. Cover with foil and bake in an oven, preheated to 400 degrees, for 25 minutes. Remove the foil then brown the top of the lasagne under a broiler for 5 minutes. Serve garnished with the chopped chervil. Time: Preparation takes about 1 hour, cooking takes about 1 hour 15 minutes.

Spinach Lasagne

Easy-cook lasagne is available, but it doesn't taste as good or cook as tender as that which you boil before baking.

SERVES 4

8 sheets green lasagne

Spinach sauce

4 Tbsps butter or margarine

4 Tbsps all-purpose flour

1¼ cups milk

3 cups frozen spinach, thawed and finely chopped

Pinch of ground nutmeg

Salt and freshly ground black pepper

Mornay Sauce

2 Tbsps butter or margarine

2 Tbsps all-purpose flour

1¼ cups milk

⅔ cup Parmesan cheese, grated

1 tsp French mustard

Salt

To make the spinach sauce, melt the butter in a pan, stir in the flour, and cook for 30 seconds. Take the pan off the heat and gradually stir in the milk. Return to the heat and bring to a boil, stirring continuously. Cook for 3 minutes, then add the spinach, nutmeg, and salt and pepper to taste. Set aside until needed.

Cook the lasagne in a large pan of boiling, salted water for 8-10 minutes, or until *al dente*. Rinse in cold water and drain well. Spread out to dry on a clean cloth.

To make the Mornay sauce, heat the butter in a pan and stir in the flour, cooking for 30 seconds. Remove from the heat, and stir in the milk. Return to the heat, stirring continuously, until boiling. Continue stirring, and simmer for 3 minutes. Add two-thirds of cheese, mustard, and salt to taste, then leave until required.

Grease an ovenproof baking dish. Line the bottom with a layer of lasagne, followed by some of the spinach mixture and a layer of cheese sauce. Repeat the process, finishing with a layer of lasagne and a covering of the cheese sauce. Scatter the remaining cheese over the lasagne. Bake in an oven, preheated to 400 degrees, for about 20-30 minutes or until golden-brown. Serve immediately.

Time: Preparation takes 10 minutes, cooking takes 30 minutes.

Cook's Tip: If the top of the lasagne does not brown sufficiently in the oven, finish it off under the broiler.

Fresh Pasta with Ceps

A wonderful recipe of intense flavor. Ceps are known in Italian as porcini. They are available fresh in season or dried in good supermarkets and gourmet food stores.

SERVES 4

1 pound fresh pasta

2 cups fresh ceps or ½ cup dried ceps

⅓ cup butter

1-2 garlic cloves, finely chopped

Salt and freshly ground black pepper

1 Tbsp freshly chopped chives

Cook the pasta in boiling, salted water until *al dente*. Drain, rinse, and set aside to drain.

Cut off the stem ends from the ceps. Wash the mushrooms carefully and dry them well, then cut into very thin slices. Heat one third of the butter and sauté the ceps with the garlic for 2 minutes. Season with plenty of salt and pepper. Add the remaining butter to the pan. When it has melted add the pasta, stir briskly, then add the chives. Cook until the pasta is heated through completely, and serve on warmed plates.

Time: Preparation takes 10 minutes, cooking takes 10 minutes.

Pasta Shells with Blue Cheese Sauce

Gorgonzola is an ideal blue cheese for cooking – it has a sharp, tangy flavor.

SERVES 4

¾ cup crumbled Gorgonzola cheese

4 Tbsps milk

2 Tbsps butter

3 Tbsps heavy cream

Salt

10 ounces pasta shells

Parmesan cheese, grated

Heat the Gorgonzola, milk, and butter gently in a saucepan. Stir with a wooden spoon to make a smooth sauce, then stir in the cream, adding a little salt if necessary.

Meanwhile, cook the pasta in plenty of boiling, salted water for 10-12 minutes, or until *al dente*. Drain, shaking the colander to remove the excess water. Add the pasta to the hot sauce and toss until well coated. Serve immediately with grated Parmesan cheese on the side.

Time: Preparation takes 5 minutes, cooking takes 15 minutes.

Tortellini

Tortellini are like little hats of filled pasta. They are always served with a sauce.

SERVES 4

Filling

2 Tbsps cream cheese

1 cooked chicken breast, finely diced

1 slice of ham, shredded

2 spinach leaves, stalks removed, cooked, and finely chopped

1 Tbsp grated Parmesan cheese

1 egg, beaten

Salt and freshly ground black pepper

Pasta dough

1¼ cups all-purpose flour

Pinch of salt

1 Tbsp water

1 Tbsp oil

3 eggs, lightly beaten

Sauce

1 cup heavy cream

1 cup mushrooms, sliced

2 Tbsps grated Parmesan cheese

1 Tbsp chopped fresh parsley

Salt and freshly ground black pepper

Beat the cream cheese until soft and smooth, then add the chicken, ham, spinach, and Parmesan cheese, and mix well. Add the egg gradually, with salt and pepper to taste. Set aside. Sift the flour and salt into a bowl and make a well in the center. Mix the water, oil, and eggs together and pour into the well, working in the flour a little at a time. Continue until the mixture comes together in a ball. Knead on a lightly floured surface for 5 minutes, or until smooth and elastic. Cover and leave to stand in a cool place for 15 minutes.

Roll the dough out as thinly as possible, either using a pasta machine or a rolling pin. Cut into circles using a 2-inch cutter and place half a teaspoon of filling in the center of each. Fold in half, pressing the edges together. Wrap each parcel around a forefinger and press the ends together very firmly.

Cook the tortellini in batches in a large pan of boiling, salted water for about 10 minutes or until *al dente*, stirring occasionally. Drain well. While the tortellini are cooking, make the sauce. Heat the cream in a saucepan. Add the mushrooms, Parmesan, parsley, and salt and pepper to taste. Gently cook for 3 minutes. Toss the sauce together with the tortellini. Serve immediately.

Time: Preparation takes 30 minutes, cooking takes 15 minutes.

Rabbit Ravioli with —Tarragon—

This is a well flavored, country dish. Chicken may be used in place of the rabbit, if preferred.

SERVES 4

3 cups all-purpose flour
4 eggs, lightly beaten
½ leek
1 onion
1 carrot
3 rabbit thigh portions
2 Tbsps olive oil
5 sprigs fresh tarragon
1 bouquet garni
Salt and freshly ground black pepper
4 Tbsps heavy cream

Place the flour in a bowl and make a well in the center. Add 3 of the eggs, mix with your fingers to make a dough, and form it into a ball. Knead until smooth then set aside to rest in a cool place for 15 minutes.

Dice the leek, onion, and carrot. Fry the rabbit in the oil until lightly browned. Remove the tarragon leaves from 3 of the sprigs, reserve the stalks for the broth, and chop the leaves. Add the onion, carrot, leek, tarragon stalks, and bouquet garni to the rabbit. Cook for 2 minutes, then add 3 cups of water. Cook, covered, over a low heat for 1½ hours, then when tender, remove the rabbit portions from the pan and take the meat off the bones. Chop it very finely and mix with ¾ of the chopped tarragon leaves, then season with salt and pepper. Strain the broth through a fine strainer and set aside.

Divide the dough into smaller, flat rounds and pass them through a pasta machine to form thin pasta strips, or roll out with a rolling pin. Cut the pasta into even-sized rectangles to make the ravioli. Mix 2 tablespoons of the rabbit broth into the meat and tarragon and place about 1 teaspoon of the mixture in the center of each piece of pasta. Brush the edges of the dough with the remaining beaten egg and fold over the filling to make the ravioli. Pinch the edges together with your fingers then, using a pastry cutter, shape into rounds. Cook the ravioli for 5 minutes in plenty of boiling, salted water with one of the remaining sprigs of tarragon. Drain with a slotted spoon. Reduce 1½ cups of the rabbit broth by half. Add the cream and remaining chopped tarragon, season to taste, and heat through. Serve the ravioli and cream sauce in soup plates. Garnish with the remaining tarragon sprig.

Time: Preparation takes 1 hour 30 minutes, cooking takes 1 hour 50 minutes.

Tortiglioni à la Puttanesca

This well-flavored dish is typical of many areas of central and southern Italy where strongly flavored ingredients such as chili, anchovies, and garlic are popular.

SERVES 4

1 cup plum tomatoes, drained
2-ounce can anchovy fillets, drained
10 ounces pasta spirals
2 Tbsps olive oil
1 clove garlic, finely chopped
Pinch of chili powder
4-5 fresh basil leaves, torn or chopped
2 Tbsps chopped fresh parsley
1/2 cup black olives, pitted and chopped
Salt and freshly ground black pepper

Chop the tomatoes and remove the seeds. Chop the anchovies. Cook the pasta in plenty of boiling, salted water for about 10-12 minutes, or until *al dente*. Rinse in hot water, drain well, and place in a warmed serving dish.

Meanwhile, heat the oil in a saucepan, add the garlic and chili powder, and cook for 1 minute. Add the tomatoes, basil, parsley, olives, and anchovies and cook for a few minutes. Season with salt and pepper. Pour the sauce over the pasta and mix together thoroughly. Serve immediately.
Time: Preparation takes 10 minutes, cooking takes 15 minutes.

Spaghetti, Egg, Bacon & Mushroom

Spaghetti, eggs, and bacon is a classic combination. The mushrooms add extra flavor.

SERVES 4

4 Tbsps butter or margarine
2 cups mushrooms, sliced
4 slices bacon, rind removed, diced
10 ounces spaghetti
Salt and freshly ground black pepper
2 eggs, hard-cooked and finely chopped
1 Tbsp chopped fresh parsley
4 Tbsps grated Parmesan cheese

Melt half the butter in a skillet, add the mushrooms and bacon, and cook for 10 minutes over a moderate heat, or until the bacon is crisp.

Meanwhile, cook the spaghetti in plenty of boiling, salted water for 10-12 minutes, or until *al dente*. Drain well and return to the pan.

Add the remaining butter, some salt, and lots of black pepper, and the mushrooms and bacon. Toss together. Serve topped with the hard-cooked eggs and chopped parsley. Serve with the grated Parmesan cheese.
Time: Preparation takes 10 minutes, cooking takes 15 minutes.

Cannelloni

Cannelloni should be cooked in a very hot oven to crisp the top of the pasta, while leaving most of the dish tender and moist.

SERVES 4

12 cannelloni tubes

Filling

1 Tbsp olive oil

2 garlic cloves, finely chopped

1 onion, chopped

2 cups ground beef

1 tsp tomato paste

1 Tbsp chopped fresh basil

1 Tbsp chopped fresh oregano

2 cups frozen spinach, thawed

1 egg, lightly beaten

4 Tbsps heavy cream

Salt and freshly ground black pepper

Tomato sauce

1 Tbsp olive oil

1 onion, chopped

1 clove garlic, finely chopped

14-ounce can chopped tomatoes

2 Tbsps tomato paste

Salt and freshly ground black pepper

Béchamel sauce

2 Tbsps butter or margarine	Salt and freshly ground black pepper
2 Tbsps all-purpose flour	2 Tbsps Parmesan cheese, grated
1¼ cups milk	3 peppercorns
1 slice of onion	1 small bayleaf

Prepare the filling. Heat the oil in a skillet, add the garlic and onion, and cook gently until soft and transparent. Add the beef and cook, stirring constantly, until well browned. Drain off any fat, add the tomato paste, basil, and oregano and cook gently for 15 minutes. Add the spinach, egg, cream, and salt and pepper to taste.

Cook the cannelloni in a large pan of boiling, salted water for 15-20 minutes, or until *al dente*. Rinse in hot water and drain well. Carefully fill the pasta tubes with the meat mixture, using a teaspoon or a piping bag with a wide, plain tip.

To make the tomato sauce, heat the oil in a pan, add the onion and garlic, and cook gently until transparent. Press the tomatoes through a strainer and add to the pan with the tomato paste and salt and pepper. Bring to a boil then simmer for 5 minutes. Set to one side.

To make the béchamel sauce, place the milk in a pan with the onion, peppercorns, and bayleaf. Heat gently for 1 minute, taking care not to boil, then set aside to cool for 5 minutes. Strain. Melt the butter in a pan. Remove it from the heat and stir in the flour then gradually add the milk. Bring to a boil, stirring continuously, until the sauce boils and thickens. Season to taste.

Spread the tomato sauce in the bottom of an ovenproof dish. Lay the cannelloni on top and cover with the béchamel sauce. Sprinkle with the grated cheese and bake in an oven preheated to 450 degrees for 10-15 minutes. Serve immediately.

Time: Preparation takes 10 minutes, cooking takes 1 hour.

Serving Idea: A hearty Italian red wine, such as Barolo, goes well with this dish.

Spaghetti à la Vongole

Vongole is the Italian word for clams, and this is a classic Neapolitan pasta dish.

SERVES 4-6

2 pounds live clams
6 Tbsps olive oil
1 pound spaghetti
2 x 14-ounce cans chopped tomatoes
2 garlic cloves, finely chopped
Salt and freshly ground black pepper
2 Tbsps chopped fresh parsley

Wash and scrub the clams, changing the water frequently as you wash. Discard any with broken shells or any open ones that will not shut when lightly tapped.

Heat the oil in a large pan, add the clams, cover, and cook for 4-5 minutes or until the shells open, shaking the pan occasionally. Lift the clams out with a slotted spoon. Remove the clams from their shells, discarding any that have not opened. Boil the cooking liquor from the clams to reduce by half, then strain through a fine strainer lined with cheesecloth.

Cook the spaghetti in plenty of boiling, salted water for 10-12 minutes, or until *al dente*. Drain, rinse in boiling water, then drain again. Meanwhile, add the tomatoes and garlic to the reduced clam liquor in a pan and heat through, seasoning to taste. Add the clams, reheat gently, then add the hot spaghetti and toss until well mixed. Serve garnished with the chopped fresh parsley.
Time: Preparation takes 30 minutes, cooking takes about 35 minutes.

Spinach Fettuccini with Cream Sauce

This dish is a simple celebration of fragrant flavors.

SERVES 4

2¼ cups all-purpose flour
2 eggs
1 cup spinach, cooked and chopped
2 Tbsps fresh chopped chives
1 cup light cream
Salt and freshly ground black pepper

Mix together the flour, eggs, and spinach in a large bowl. Mix well and form the dough into a ball. Knead lightly, then sprinkle the dough with flour and set aside in the refrigerator for 30 minutes.

Roll out the dough with a rolling pin or pass it through the rollers of a pasta machine and then cut it into fettuccini. Spread the strips out on a floured surface; the strips should not touch one another. Allow to dry for a few minutes.

Bring a large pan of salted water to a boil, add the pasta, and cook for a few minutes until *al dente*. Rinse under hot water and set aside to drain.

Heat together the chives and cream, without boiling, add the pasta to the pan, stir well, and serve when the pasta is heated through. Season with a little salt and pepper if necessary.
Time: Preparation takes 40 minutes, plus chilling. Cooking takes 20 minutes.

Meat Ravioli with -Red Peppers-

Red bell peppers are used to color the pasta and flavor the sauce for this innovative dish.

SERVES 4

2 red bell peppers,
2 cups all-purpose flour
2 eggs, lightly beaten
1 cup ground beef
1 Tbsp chopped fresh parsley
½ onion, chopped
Salt and freshly ground black pepper
½ cup light cream
⅓ cup butter

Remove the seeds and core from the red bell peppers. Roughly chop the flesh then place in a food processor and blend until liquid. Transfer to a small bowl and set aside until the pulp rises to the surface. This takes about 30 minutes.

To make the pasta dough, place the flour in a bowl, make a well in the center, add 1 of the eggs and 3 tablespoons of the red bell pepper pulp (not the juice.) Mix thoroughly and form into a ball. Knead lightly until smooth then set the dough aside for 30 minutes.

Mix together the meat, parsley, and onion and season with salt and pepper. Roll the dough out very thinly, using a pasta machine or a rolling pin. Cut the dough into a even number of equal-sized rectangles. Place the stuffing on half of the strips in little piles about 1½ inches apart. Beat the remaining egg and use it to brush around the filling.

Cover with the remaining pasta dough. Cut into ravioli shapes using a cookie cutter, and press the edges together well to seal.

Bring a large saucepan of salted water to a boil and cook the ravioli for about 3 minutes or until they float to the top of the water. While the ravioli are cooking, prepare the sauce by heating the cream with ½ cup of the red bell pepper pulp. Bring to a boil and then gradually whisk in the butter. Drain the ravioli. Serve the pasta with the hot cream sauce poured over it.

Time: Preparation takes 50 minutes, plus resting time for the pasta. Cooking takes 15 minutes.

Variation: Add a teaspoon of wine vinegar and a few drops of Tabasco sauce to the bell pepper sauce to give a peppery flavor.

Meat Ravioli

Ravioli are little parcels of pasta traditionally filled with meat.

SERVES 4

Filling

4 Tbsps butter or margarine

1 clove garlic, finely chopped

1 onion, grated

1 cup ground beef

5 Tbsps red wine

Salt and freshly ground black pepper

2 Tbsps bread crumbs

1 cup cooked spinach, chopped

2 eggs, beaten

Pasta dough

2 cups all-purpose flour

3 eggs, lightly beaten

Sauce

14-ounce can chopped tomatoes

1 small onion, grated

1 small carrot, finely diced

1 bayleaf

2 parsley stalks

Salt and freshly ground black pepper

Heat the butter in a pan, add the garlic and onion, and fry gently for 1 minute. Add the ground beef and fry until browned. Add the red wine, some salt and pepper, and cook, uncovered, for 15 minutes. Strain off the juices and reserve for the sauce. Allow the filling to cool then add the bread crumbs, spinach, and the eggs to bind. Add salt and pepper to taste. Set aside.

Sieve the flour into a bowl. Make a well in the center and add the eggs. Work the flour and eggs together with a fork then knead by hand, until a smooth dough is formed. Cover the dough and leave to rest for 15 minutes in a cool place.

Lightly flour a board, divide the dough in two, and roll out thinly into even-sized rectangles, using a pasta machine or rolling pin. Place small piles of the filling about 1½ inches apart on one half of the dough. Place the remaining dough on top and cut with a ravioli cutter or small cookie cutter. Seal the edges by pinching together. Cook the ravioli in batches in a large, wide pan with plenty of boiling, salted water for about 8 minutes or until *al dente*. Remove the ravioli carefully with a slotted spoon.

Meanwhile, place all the ingredients for the sauce in a saucepan. Add the reserved juice from the cooked meat and bring to a boil. Simmer for 10 minutes. Press the sauce through a sieve and return the smooth sauce to the pan. Adjust the seasoning. Place the drained ravioli in a warmed serving dish and cover with the sauce. Serve immediately.

Time: Preparation takes 30 minutes, cooking takes 30 minutes.

Spinach Ravioli

Spinach makes an unusual but tasty filling for ravioli.

SERVES 4

Filling

2 cups cooked spinach, well drained

2 Tbsps butter or margarine

4 Tbsps Parmesan cheese, grated

Pinch of grated nutmeg

Salt and freshly ground black pepper

1 egg, beaten

Dough

2¼ cups all-purpose flour

3 eggs, lightly beaten

Cheese sauce

2 Tbsps butter or margarine

3 Tbsps all-purpose flour

1¼ cups milk

1 tsp French mustard

2 Tbsps grated Parmesan cheese

Chop the spinach and heat it in a pan, then beat in the butter. Add the Parmesan cheese, nutmeg, and salt and freshly ground black pepper to taste. Finally mix in the beaten egg. Set aside until required.

Sift the flour into a bowl, make a well in the center, and add the eggs. Work the flour and the eggs together with a fork and then knead by hand until a smooth dough is formed. Cover and leave to rest for 15 minutes.

Lightly flour a work surface, divide the dough in half, and roll out thinly into two even-sized rectangles by hand or using a pasta machine. Shape the filling into small balls and set them about 1½ inches apart on one piece of the dough. Place the other half on top and cut with a ravioli cutter or small cookie cutter. Seal the edges with a fork. Cook in batches in a large pan of boiling, salted water for about 8 minutes, or until *al dente*. Remove the ravioli carefully with a slotted spoon.

Meanwhile, heat the butter in a pan. Add the flour and cook, stirring, for 30 seconds. Take the pan off the heat and gradually stir in the milk. Bring to a boil, stirring continuously, and simmer for 3 minutes. Add the mustard, half the cheese, and some seasoning to taste. Pour the sauce over the ravioli and serve immediately with the remaining cheese sprinkled over the top.
Time: Preparation takes 30 minutes, cooking takes 20 minutes.

Lasagne

Lasagne, a glorious dish of layered pasta, meat sauce, and fragrant white sauce, is best made with fresh pasta. If using dried, choose a lasagne that requires pre-cooking – it only takes a few minutes and the flavor is so much better than the no-cook variety.

SERVES 4

8 sheets lasagne

Meat sauce

4 Tbsps butter or margarine

1 onion, chopped

1 stick celery, sliced

2 carrots, diced

½ cup ground beef

1 Tbsp all-purpose flour

1 Tbsp tomato paste

⅔ cup beef broth

1 tsp chopped fresh marjoram

Salt and freshly ground black pepper

Béchamel sauce

1¼ cups milk

6 black peppercorns

Slice of onion

1 bayleaf

Parsley stalks

4 Tbsps butter or margarine

3 Tbsps all-purpose flour

Heat the butter for the meat sauce in a skillet, add the onion, celery, and carrots, and cook until the onion is golden. Add the ground beef and brown well, then stir in the flour, tomato paste, beef broth, marjoram, and salt and black pepper. Simmer for 15 minutes.

Meanwhile, cook the lasagne in plenty of boiling, salted water for 10 minutes, or until *al dente*. Rinse in cold water and drain well. Spread the lasagne out on a cloth to dry.

Bring the milk almost to a boil in a saucepan with the peppercorns, onion, bayleaf, and parsley stalks. Remove from the heat, leave to cool for 5 minutes, then strain through a strainer to remove the flavorings. Melt the butter in a saucepan, then stir in the flour and cook for 30 seconds. Remove the pan from the heat and gradually add the milk, stirring continuously. Bring to a boil, then simmer for 3 minutes.

Grease an ovenproof baking dish. Line the bottom with a layer of lasagne. Cover with a layer of meat sauce, then a layer of béchamel sauce. Add another layer of lasagne and repeat the layers until all the ingredients are used, finishing with a layer of béchamel sauce. Bake in an oven, preheated to 400 degrees, for about 20 minutes, or until the top is golden. Serve immediately. Time: Preparation takes 10 minutes, cooking takes 45 minutes.

Macaroni Cheese with —Anchovies—

Anchovies give an extra flavor dimension to macaroni cheese.

SERVES 4

2-ounce can anchovy fillets

8 ounces macaroni

4 Tbsps butter or margarine

4 Tbsps all-purpose flour

2½ cups milk

½ tsp mustard powder

¾ cup grated Swiss or Cheddar cheese

Salt and freshly ground black pepper

Drain the anchovies, reserving 4-5 fillets to make a thin lattice over the dish. Chop the rest finely. Cook the macaroni in plenty of boiling, salted water for 10-12 minutes, or until *al dente*. Rinse in hot water and drain well.

Meanwhile, melt the butter in a pan, stir in the flour, and cook for 1 minute. Remove from the heat and gradually stir in the milk. Return to the heat and bring to a boil, stirring continuously. Simmer for 3 minutes, then stir in the mustard, chopped anchovies, and half the cheese. Season with salt and pepper to taste, then stir in the macaroni and pour into an ovenproof dish. Scatter the remaining cheese over the top and make a lattice with the sliced anchovies. Brown under a preheated hot broiler, and serve immediately.

Time: Preparation takes 5 minutes, cooking takes 15 minutes.

Variation: Try using whole-wheat macaroni for a change of flavor.

Fettuccini with Creamy – Liver Sauce –

Chicken livers make an unusual but delicious accompaniment to pasta.

SERVES 4

2 medium onions, sliced

1 clove garlic, finely chopped

4 Tbsps olive oil

½ cup sliced mushrooms

2 cups chicken livers, cleaned and sliced

½ cup light cream

2 eggs, beaten

Salt and freshly ground black pepper

10 ounces fettuccini

Olive oil

1 Tbsp chopped fresh parsley

In a large skillet, cook the onions and garlic gently in the oil until softened. Add the mushrooms and cook for 3 minutes. Add the chicken livers to the pan and cook until lightly browned. Remove from the heat and stir in the cream. Return to a low heat and cook, uncovered, for a further 2 minutes without boiling. Remove from the heat, and stir in the lightly beaten eggs. Season with salt and pepper to taste.

Meanwhile, cook the fettuccini in plenty of boiling, salted water for 10-12 minutes, or until *al dente*. Drain the fettuccini and toss in a little olive oil and black pepper. Serve the sauce over the pasta and sprinkle with the parsley.

Time: Preparation takes 10 minutes, cooking takes 15 minutes.

Cook's Tip: Be careful not to over-cook the livers as they will toughen.

Pasta Spirals, Blue Cheese & Walnuts

Walnuts and blue cheese make a perfect flavor combination in this delicious pasta sauce.

SERVES 4

1 pound pasta spirals

1¼ cups heavy cream

1 pound blue cheese

1 cup walnut halves

Freshly ground black pepper

4 sprigs fresh thyme, to garnish

2 ripe figs, to garnish

Cook the pasta in plenty of boiling, salted water for 10-12 minutes, or until *al dente*.

Meanwhile, place the heavy cream in a saucepan and bring to a boil. Boil rapidly for 3 minutes, then crumble in the cheese and stir until the cheese melts. Stir in the walnut halves and season with pepper.

When the pasta is cooked, drain it well, then return it to the pan. Pour the sauce over the pasta and mix well. Serve each portion garnished with sprigs of thyme and half a ripe fig.

Time: Preparation takes 5 minutes, cooking takes about 15 minutes.

Variation: The walnut sauce makes a superb dipping sauce.

Macaroni au Gratin

This is a typical Mediterranean dish, and a very good way of turning just a little meat into a satisfying meal for four.

SERVES 4

1 pound macaroni

4 Tbsps butter

1 cup ground lamb

Salt and freshly ground black pepper

½ cup grated Parmesan cheese

3 Tbsps bread crumbs

Cook the macaroni in boiling, salted water for 10-12 minutes, or until *al dente*. Rinse in boiling water, then set aside to drain.

Melt the butter in a skillet and fry the lamb rapidly, seasoning it with salt and black pepper. Place a layer of macaroni in the bottom of a greased ovenproof dish and then a layer of cheese. Sprinkle the meat over the cheese and then cover the meat with another layer of macaroni. Sprinkle over another layer of cheese and then all the bread crumbs. Bake in an oven preheated to 400 degrees, for 20-30 minutes. Serve immediately.

Time: Preparation takes 15 minutes, cooking takes 50 minutes.

Pasta al Forno

Al Forno means baked in the oven, so this is oven-baked pasta.

SERVES 4

8 ounces macaroni

4 Tbsps butter or margarine

4 Tbsps Parmesan cheese, grated

Pinch of grated nutmeg

Salt and freshly ground black pepper

2 eggs, beaten

1 medium onion, chopped

1 clove garlic, finely chopped

2 cups ground beef

2 Tbsps tomato paste

⅓ cup beef broth

2 Tbsps chopped fresh parsley

4 Tbsps red wine

2 Tbsps all-purpose flour

⅓ cup milk

Cook the macaroni in plenty of boiling salted water for 10-12 minutes, or until *al dente*. Rinse under hot water and drain. Place one third of the butter in the pan and return the macaroni to it. Add half the cheese, the nutmeg, and salt and pepper to taste and leave to cool. Mix in half the beaten egg and set aside.

Melt half the remaining butter in a pan, and fry the onion and garlic gently until the onion is soft. Increase the heat, add the meat, and fry until browned. Add the tomato paste, broth, parsley, and wine, and season with salt and pepper. Simmer for 20 minutes.

Melt the rest of the butter in a small pan. Stir in the flour and cook for 30 seconds, then remove from the heat and gradually stir in the milk. Bring to a boil, stirring continuously until the sauce thickens. Beat in the remaining egg and season to taste.

Spoon half the macaroni into a serving dish and cover with the meat sauce. Add another layer of macaroni, then add the white sauce, top with remaining cheese, and bake in an oven preheated to 375 degrees for 30 minutes, or until golden-brown. Serve immediately.

Time: Preparation takes 10 minutes, cooking takes 1 hour.

Macaroni with Creamy Chicken Sauce

The addition of even a little chopped chicken turns a lunchtime dish of macaroni cheese into a substantial entrée.

SERVES 4

1 Tbsp olive oil
1 small boneless chicken breast
8 ounces macaroni
4 Tbsps butter
2 Tbsps all-purpose flour
2¹/₂ cups milk
Salt and freshly ground black pepper
4 ounces mozzarella cheese, chopped or thinly sliced

Heat the oil in a skillet and gently fry the chicken breasts for 10-15 minutes, or until cooked through. Allow to cool, then shred the chicken. Cook the macaroni in plenty of boiling, salted water for 10-12 minutes, or until *al dente*. Rinse in hot water and drain well.

Meanwhile, heat the butter in a saucepan, stir in the flour and cook for 1 minute. Remove from the heat and gradually stir in the milk. Bring the sauce to a boil, stirring continuously, and cook for 3 minutes. Add the chicken, macaroni, and salt and pepper to taste, and mix well. Pour the mixture into an ovenproof dish and top with the cheese. Cook under a preheated broiler until golden-brown, then serve immediately.

Time: Preparation takes 5 minutes, cooking takes 20 minutes.

Sicilian Cannelloni

Cannelloni should be cooked in quite a small dish, so that the tops become crisp but the rest of the filled pasta remains soft and moist.

SERVES 4

16 cannelloni shells
4 Tbsps butter
1 shallot, chopped
4 mushrooms, chopped
2 slices ham, chopped
1¹/₂ cups ground beef chuck
Salt and freshly ground black pepper
10 thin slices of mozzarella cheese
¹/₂ cup chicken broth

Cook the cannelloni in a large pan of boiling, salted, water for 10-15 minutes. Rinse in hot water then set aside to drain.

Melt the butter in a saucepan and cook the shallot, mushrooms, ham, and beef for about 10 minutes. Season with salt and pepper and set aside to cool. Once cooled, fill the cannelloni with the mixture and place in a lightly greased, ovenproof dish. Place the slices of mozzarella over the cannelloni and then pour in the chicken broth.

Bake the cannelloni in an oven preheated to 400 degrees for about 15-20 minutes, or until the filling is heated through and the top is crisp and golden. Serve piping hot.

Time: Preparation takes 15 minutes, cooking takes about 40 minutes.

Lasagne Napoletana

Lasagne as eaten in Napoli – with a simple tomato sauce. A great vegetarian dish.

SERVES 6

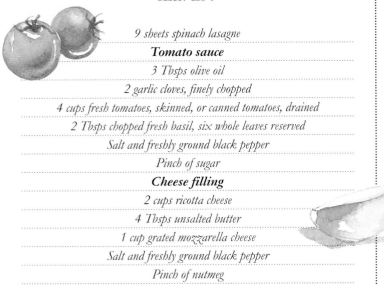

9 sheets spinach lasagne

Tomato sauce

3 Tbsps olive oil

2 garlic cloves, finely chopped

4 cups fresh tomatoes, skinned, or canned tomatoes, drained

2 Tbsps chopped fresh basil, six whole leaves reserved

Salt and freshly ground black pepper

Pinch of sugar

Cheese filling

2 cups ricotta cheese

4 Tbsps unsalted butter

1 cup grated mozzarella cheese

Salt and freshly ground black pepper

Pinch of nutmeg

Cook the pasta for 10 minutes in boiling, salted water. Drain and rinse under hot water and place in a single layer on a damp kitchen towel until required.

Heat the oil in a large saucepan, add the garlic, and cook for 1 minute. Add the tomatoes, basil, some salt and pepper, and the sugar. Simmer for 35 minutes. Add more seasoning or sugar to taste.

Meanwhile, beat the ricotta cheese and butter together until creamy, then stir in the remaining filling ingredients.

To assemble the lasagne, grease a rectangular ovenproof dish and place 3 sheets of lasagne in the bottom. Cover with one third of the tomato sauce and carefully add half the cheese filling in a layer. Place another 3 sheets of pasta over the cheese and cover with another third of the tomato sauce. Add the remaining cheese filling and cover with the remaining lasagne. Spoon the remaining tomato sauce on top. Cover the dish with aluminum foil and bake in an oven preheated to 375 degrees, for 20 minutes. Uncover and cook for a further 10 minutes. Garnish with the reserved basil leaves before serving.

Time: Preparation takes 25 minutes, cooking takes 1-1¼ hours.

Cook's Tip: Lasagne can be assembled a day ahead and refrigerated. Ensure it is at room temperature before cooking.

Pasta Spirals & Kidneys in Marsala Sauce

Kidneys are not often used to their full potential. Cooked with plenty of black pepper, bacon, mushrooms, and Marsala they make a delicious pasta dish.

SERVES 4

4 lambs' kidneys
Salt and freshly ground black pepper
1 Tbsp all-purpose flour
4 Tbsps butter or margarine
1 small onion, finely chopped
1 clove garlic, finely chopped
3 slices bacon, rind removed, diced
½ cup button mushrooms, sliced
⅓ cup Marsala, or dry white wine
10 ounces pasta spirals

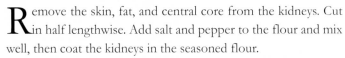

Remove the skin, fat, and central core from the kidneys. Cut in half lengthwise. Add salt and pepper to the flour and mix well, then coat the kidneys in the seasoned flour.

Heat the butter in a skillet, add the onion and garlic, and cook until soft but not browned. Add the kidneys and brown all over. Add the bacon and mushrooms and cook, stirring frequently, for 3 minutes, then add the Marsala and bring to a boil. Simmer gently for 15 minutes, or until the kidneys are tender. Add seasoning to taste.

Meanwhile, cook the pasta spirals in plenty of boiling, salted water for 10-12 minutes, or until *al dente*. Rinse in hot water and drain well. Divide the pasta between the serving dishes and spoon the kidneys on top.

Time: Preparation takes 15 minutes, cooking takes 30 minutes.

Farfalle with Mushrooms, Beef & Cream

This luxurious dish combines a prime cut of steak with the pasta and mushrooms to make a little beef go a long way.

SERVES 2-3

8 ounces fillet steak

2 Tbsps unsalted butter

1 onion, sliced

1 cup mushrooms, sliced

1 Tbsp all-purpose flour

4 Tbsps sour cream

10 green olives, pitted and chopped

Salt and freshly ground black pepper

10 ounces farfalle (pasta bows)

Garnish

Sour cream

1 Tbsp chopped fresh parsley

Cut the meat into small, thin slices, across the grain. Heat half the butter in a skillet and sauté the meat over a high heat until well browned. Remove the meat with a slotted spoon and set aside.

Heat the remaining butter in the pan, add the onion, and gently fry until soft and just beginning to color. Add the mushrooms and cook for 3 minutes, then stir in the flour and heat for a further 3 minutes. Gradually stir in the sour cream, then return the meat to the pan along with the olives and salt and pepper to taste.

Meanwhile, cook the farfalle in plenty of boiling, salted water for 10-12 minutes, or until *al dente*. Drain well. Serve the pasta with the beef and mushroom sauce on top. Garnish with sour cream and chopped parsley.

Time: Preparation takes 10 minutes, cooking takes 15 minutes.

Cook's Tip: Ensure the pasta is well drained otherwise it will spoil the consistency of the sauce.

Side Dishes

Pasta is most frequently eaten as a side dish, the mild flavor of pasta making a perfect foil to strongly-flavored meats, seafood, or fish. Instead of plain boiled spaghetti or noodles, we invite you to try some exciting variations, simple and quick enough to prepare for every day but quite delicious enough to serve to company and earn a few compliments and requests for the recipe.

The choice here ranges from exotic South Sea Noodles (page 92), and Noodles with Ginger and Oyster Sauce (page 96), both Chinese-inspired, to Noodle Vegetable Ring (page 91). Then from the eastern European pasta tradition, there is Noodle Kugel (page 94), a hearty Jewish dish, oven-baked and served mainly in winter with slow-cooked stews. New combinations, based on combining popular ingredients with noodles, include Noodles with Peppers and Ginger (page 96). In this section, we have tried to use as wide a variety of shapes as possible, to help to inspire you to find interesting ways of serving your favorite pasta shapes as side dishes, to accompany entrées.

When you serve these pasta dishes on the side, you need to be sure you are making good combinations. The Chinese-inspired pastas work well with meats such as chicken, quail, Cornish rock game hen, and turkey, as well as fish. Naturally, for a Chinese meal, noodles are just as important as rice. Side dishes containing ground meats go well with a roast, steak, or cutlet of the same meat. Vegetarian side dishes will combine with anything, including a vegetarian entrée.

All of these side dishes would make great meals on their own, perhaps served with a green salad and extra grated or shredded cheese. Vary the portion sizes. You can count on requiring half the amount of pasta for a side dish serving as for an entrée serving.

South Sea Noodles

A Chinese dish of noodles with an attractive and tasty garnish.

SERVES 3-4

2 Tbsps Chinese dried shrimp, soaked

8 ounces Chinese egg noodles

4 Tbsps oil

2 medium onions, sliced

4 slices bacon, rind removed, and chopped

2 Tbsps curry powder

Salt

⅔ cup chicken broth

Garnish

2 Tbsps oil

2 garlic cloves, chopped

1 cup peeled shrimp

1 Tbsp soy sauce

1 Tbsp Hoisin sauce

1 Tbsp pale dry sherry

4 green onions (scallions), chopped

2 Tbsps chopped fresh parsley

Drain the soaked shrimp and chop them. Cook the noodles in boiling, salted water for 3 minutes, then drain and rinse under cold water.

Heat the oil in a wok, add the onions, bacon, and chopped shrimp. Stir-fry for 1 minute, then add the curry powder and some salt. Stir-fry for a further minute. Add the broth and drained noodles. Stir-fry over the heat for 2-3 minutes, then transfer to a heated serving platter.

For the garnish, heat the oil in a small pan, add the garlic and shrimp, and stir-fry over a high heat for 1 minute. Add the soy sauce, Hoisin sauce, and sherry. Sprinkle with the green onions (scallions) and parsley and pour the sauce over the noodles to serve.

Time: Preparation takes 15 minutes, cooking takes about 20 minutes.

Noodles with Ginger & Oyster Sauce

This makes a very good accompaniment to any Chinese meat or chicken dishes, but is also a tasty snack on its own.

SERVES 2-4

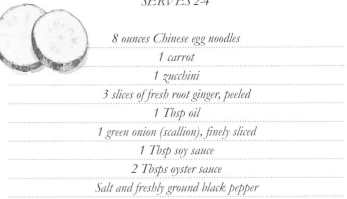

8 ounces Chinese egg noodles

1 carrot

1 zucchini

3 slices of fresh root ginger, peeled

1 Tbsp oil

1 green onion (scallion), finely sliced

1 Tbsp soy sauce

2 Tbsps oyster sauce

Salt and freshly ground black pepper

Cook the noodles in boiling, salted water as directed on the packet, then rinse under cold water and set aside to drain.

Cut the carrot into thin strips. Thickly peel the zucchini to include a little of the flesh, and cut the peel into thin strips. Discard the center of the zucchini. Cut the slices of ginger into thin strips, using a very sharp knife.

Heat the oil in a wok, and stir-fry the green onion (scallion) for 10 seconds; add the carrot, zucchini, and ginger, and stir-fry briefly. Stir in the noodles and cook for 1 minute. Stir in the soy and oyster sauces, and continue cooking until heated through. Season with salt and pepper.

Time: Preparation takes 15 minutes, cooking takes 15 minutes.

Variation: Cook the noodles in chicken broth to give them extra flavor.

Garnished Noodles

Noodles are far more interesting to serve with a Chinese meal than plain rice.

SERVES 4

3 Tbsps white wine vinegar

3 Tbsps soy sauce

2 tsps sugar

²/₃ cup chicken broth

1 pound Chinese egg noodles

Garnishes

Cucumber, diced

¹/₂ cup cooked, peeled shrimp

Celery leaves

2 sheets nori, toasted and crumbled or shredded

Combine the vinegar, soy sauce, sugar, and broth in a pan and bring to a boil. Remove from the heat and keep warm. Cook the noodles in plenty of boiling water for about 5 minutes, until tender. Drain in a colander and rinse with hot water. Divide the noodles among 4 serving dishes and arrange the garnishes on top. Pour the sauce over the noodles and serve.

Time: Preparation takes 10 minutes, cooking takes about 10 minutes.

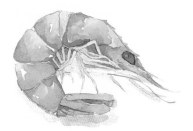

Noodle Kugel

These baked noodles are a traditional Jewish accompaniment to a Sabbath stew. They are cooked for a very long time and become light and fragrant.

SERVES 8

2 Tbsps bread crumbs

8 ounces egg noodles, cooked and drained

³/₄ cup chicken fat or butter

¹/₂ tsp salt

¹/₂ tsp black pepper

2 eggs, lightly beaten

Grease a large casserole or baking dish and sprinkle with the bread crumbs. Combine the remaining ingredients in a large bowl, then pour into the prepared dish, and cover tightly with foil. Bake in an oven, preheated to 450 degrees, for 30 minutes, then reduce the heat to 375 degrees and bake for another 30 minutes. Reduce heat further to 200 degrees and cook for at least 4 more hours. Serve with stew or other meats.

Time: Preparation takes about 15 minutes, cooking takes 5 hours.

Spicy Oriental Noodles

This dish is delicious with sliced cold meat or chicken.

SERVES 4

8 ounces Chinese egg noodles (medium thickness)

5 Tbsps oil

4 carrots

2 cups broccoli flowerets

12 dried shiitake mushrooms, soaked in warm water for 30 minutes

4 green onions (scallions), sliced diagonally

1 clove garlic

1-2 tsps chili sauce, mild or hot

4 Tbsps soy sauce

4 Tbsps rice wine or dry sherry

2 tsps cornstarch

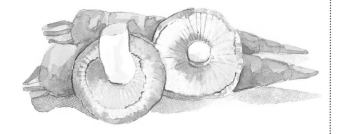

Cook the noodles in boiling, salted water for about 4-5 minutes. Drain well, then rinse under hot water, and drain again. Toss with about 1 tablespoon of the oil to prevent them sticking together.

Slice the carrots thinly on the diagonal. Blanch the carrot and broccoli in boiling water for about 2 minutes then drain, rinse under cold water, and leave to drain. Remove and discard the mushroom stems and slice the caps thinly. Set aside with the green onions (scallions).

Heat a wok and add the remaining oil with the garlic clove. Leave the garlic in the pan while the oil heats and then remove and discard it. Add the carrots and broccoli and stir-fry for about 1 minute. Add the sliced mushrooms and green onions (scallions) and continue to stir-fry, tossing the vegetables in the pan continuously.

Combine the chili sauce, soy sauce, wine, and cornstarch, mixing well. Pour the mixture over the vegetables in the wok and cook until the sauce boils and clears. Add the noodles, toss with the vegetables, and heat through. Serve immediately.

Time: Preparation takes 25 minutes, cooking takes about 8 minutes.

Variation: To turn this dish into a main course, simply add meat or shrimp and stir-fry before adding the vegetables.

Noodles with Peppers & Ginger

This is a very fragrant way of cooking noodles. Cutting the peppers very finely releases the flavor more effectively.

SERVES 4

1 red bell pepper

1 green bell pepper

8 ounces Chinese egg noodles

1 Tbsp oil

1 tsp finely chopped fresh root ginger

1 clove garlic, finely chopped

Salt and freshly ground black pepper

Cut the top and bottom off the peppers. Cut through one side of each and open the peppers out flat, removing the seeds and cores. Cut the pepper flesh into six pieces. Cut each of these pieces in half, crosswise, through the flesh, to form wide, thin slices. Cut each slice into very thin matchsticks.

Cook the noodles until just tender in boiling, salted water, stirring occasionally so that they do not stick. Drain the noodles in a strainer and rinse under cold running water. Set aside to drain.

Heat the oil in a wok and stir-fry the peppers, ginger, and garlic for 1 minute, stirring continuously. Add the well-drained noodles and stir-fry until the noodles are hot. Season to taste and serve immediately.

Time: Preparation takes 15 minutes, cooking takes about 10 minutes.

Braised Noodles

You will need a large napkin to protect your clothing while you enjoy this dish!

SERVES 4

8 ounces Chinese egg noodles

3 Tbsps oil

6 green onions (scallions), chopped

1 small piece fresh root ginger, grated

1¼ cups chicken or vegetable broth

2 Tbsps soy sauce

Garnishes

2 red chilies, seeded and finely chopped

2 Tbsps chopped fresh coriander (cilantro)

4 Tbsps roasted peanuts, chopped

Cook the noodles in boiling, salted water until just tender. Drain them and rinse under hot water. Toss in a colander to remove excess water.

Heat the oil in a wok or heavy-based pan and cook the green onions (scallions) and ginger for about 1 minute. Add the noodles and fry on one side until golden-brown. Turn over and fry on the other side until golden.

Mix the broth and soy sauce together, and gradually pour over the noodles. Simmer for 5 minutes, stirring occasionally. Serve in individual bowls, sprinkled with the garnishes.

Time: Preparation takes 15 minutes, cooking takes 15 minutes.

Noodle Vegetable Ring

An unusual way of serving fettuccini. Pack the noodles firmly into the tube-pan, so that they will release easily for serving.

SERVES 4-6

3 ounces egg noodles or thin fettuccini
Oil
3 Tbsps butter or margarine
3 Tbsps all-purpose flour
1½ cups milk
Salt, freshly ground black pepper and paprika
1 cup grated Cheddar cheese
2 eggs, beaten
¼ cup mixed peas and carrots, cooked
½ cup broccoli flowerets, cooked
½ cup sweetcorn, cooked
1 small red bell pepper, diced

Cook the egg noodles in a large pan of boiling, salted water until tender. Drain well and toss with a little oil to prevent them from sticking.

Melt the butter in a saucepan, then stir in the flour. Cook for about 1 minute, then gradually beat in the milk until smooth. Add a good pinch of salt, pepper, and paprika. Bring to a boil, stirring continuously, and cook until thick. Add the cheese and stir until melted. Divide the sauce in two.

Add half the sauce and the eggs to the noodles and mix thoroughly. Spoon the mixture into a well-greased tube-pan. Place the tube-pan in a roasting pan containing enough hot water to come halfway up the sides of the tube-pan. Bake in an oven preheated to 350 degrees, for about 45 minutes, or until completely set.

Meanwhile, combine the cooked vegetables with the diced pepper and the remaining cheese sauce. If the sauce is too thick, add a little more milk. Unmold the noodle ring on to a large platter and sprinkle with paprika. Spoon the vegetables in their sauce into the middle and serve.

Time: Preparation takes 20 minutes, cooking takes about 1 hour.

Singapore Fried Noodles

There is plenty of everything in the busy cosmopolitan port of Singapore and the cooking is a rich mixture of many ingredients.

SERVES 4

8 ounces egg noodles

3 Tbsps oil

2 eggs, lightly beaten

Salt and freshly ground black pepper

2 garlic cloves, finely chopped

1 tsp chili powder

1 chicken breast, cut into shreds

3 sticks celery, sliced diagonally

2 green onions (scallions), sliced

1 red chili, seeded and sliced

1 green chili, seeded and sliced

2 cups shrimp, peeled and deveined

1/2 cup beansprouts

Soak the noodles in boiling water for 8 minutes, or as directed on the packet. Drain and leave to dry, spread out on a clean tea-towel.

Heat a wok and add 1 tablespoon of the oil. Add the lightly beaten eggs and salt and pepper to taste, stir gently, then cook until set. Remove from the wok and cut into thin strips and keep warm.

Add the remaining oil to the wok. When hot, add the garlic and chili powder, and fry for 30 seconds, then add the chicken, celery, green onions (scallions), and red and green chilies and stir-fry for 8 minutes, or until chicken has cooked through. Add the noodles, shrimp, and beansprouts and toss until well mixed and heated through. Serve with the egg strips on top.

Time: Preparation takes 20 minutes, cooking takes about 20 minutes.

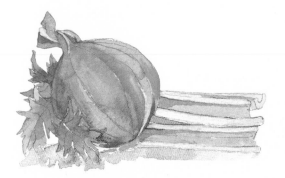

Spicy Fried Noodles

This recipe may be made with thread egg noodles or the thin, flat *mie* noodles, which are like linguini.

SERVES 4

8 ounces Chinese egg noodles

3 Tbsps oil

1 medium onion, finely chopped

2 garlic cloves, finely chopped

1 small piece fresh root ginger, grated

1/2 tsp ground cumin

1/2 tsp ground coriander (cilantro)

1/4 tsp ground nutmeg

1/4 tsp ground cinnamon

1/4 tsp cayenne pepper

1/4 cup soy sauce

Salt and freshly ground black pepper

Garnish

1 omelet, cut into strips

1 stick celery, very thinly shredded

Cook the noodles in boiling, salted water until just tender. Drain and refresh under hot water, tossing in a colander to remove excess water.

Heat the oil in a large, heavy-based skillet or wok, and fry the onion, garlic, and ginger until softened. Add the spices and cook for 2 minutes. Stir in the noodles and then fry over a gentle heat for about 3 minutes. Add the soy sauce and season with salt and pepper. Serve topped with the garnishes.

Time: Preparation takes 10 minutes, cooking takes about 20 minutes.

Desserts

Pasta is not normally thought of as a dessert ingredient, which is why these dessert recipes are so exciting and unusual. Pasta adds a most unusual touch to a dessert. However, you will need to plan your meal carefully. Pasta is considered rather filling for dessert purposes so you should ensure that the entrée is fairly light and nothing in it will "clash" with your dessert idea.

Among the mouth-watering desserts featured are Black Cherry Ravioli with Sour Cream Sauce (page102), Peach Brûlée (page 105) and a variation on the Chinese eight-treasure rice dessert called Eight Treasure Macaroni (page 106).

Pasta makes a great dessert base, instead of graham cracker crumbs or pastry dough. Use strips of cooked fettuccini or noodles and arrange them in a thickly-buttered bowl, angel-cake pan, or tube-pan. Add a thick fruity filling or jello to the center, and refrigerate until set. Unmold onto a large plate just before serving. If you are using macaroni and a bowl for the mold, the result will look something like an old-fashioned beehive, so you could pour a little liquid honey on it, and attach a couple of furry bee decorations!

You can easily concoct your own finales to the meal, using our pasta ideas as the base and adding your own fruits in season. What about a pasta-and-cranberry dessert for Thanksgiving, for instance? Pasta desserts are an unusual surprise for a kids' party. Our Vanilla Cream Melba (page 106) would make a great party treat, using unusual pasta shapes.

Since pasta desserts are so filling, they are often best served as a snack between meals, instead of cake or cookies. A slice of Creamy Macaroni with Apricot Purée (page 105) with a cup of coffee in late afternoon would prove popular with most people – except perhaps dieters!

Cherry Ravioli with Sour Cream Sauce

Ravioli may be savory or sweet – these are filled with tart black cherries.

SERVES 4

Dough
2¼ cups all-purpose flour

1 Tbsp sugar

3 eggs, lightly beaten

Filling and sauce
1-pound can pitted black cherries, drained and juice reserved

2 Tbsps sugar

1 tsp potato starch

½ cup sour cream

½ cup heavy cream

Sift the flour and sugar into a mixing bowl. Make a well in the center and add the lightly-beaten eggs. Work the flour and eggs together with a spoon and then by hand, until a dough is formed. Knead gently until smooth and shiny. Wrap and leave in a cool place for 15 minutes.

Divide the dough in half. Lightly flour a board and roll the dough out thinly into two even-sized rectangles, using a rolling pin or a pasta machine. Cut the dough in half. Place the well-drained cherries about 1½ inches apart on the dough. Place the other half on top and cut out the ravioli with a small glass or cookie cutter. Seal well around the edges with the back of a fork. Boil plenty of water in a large saucepan, then drop in the cherry pasta. Cook for about 10 minutes, or until they rise to the surface. Remove with a draining spoon and keep warm.

Reserve 2 tablespoons of the cherry juice and mix the remaining juice with the sugar in a saucepan. Set over a medium heat to dissolve the sugar. Mix 1 tablespoon of the reserved juice with the potato starch, add to the pan, and heat until it boils and thickens, stirring constantly.

Meanwhile, mix the sour cream and heavy cream together and marble the remaining 1 tablespoon of cherry juice through it. Pour the hot, thickened cherry juice over the cherry ravioli. Serve hot, with the cream sauce.

Time: Preparation takes 30 minutes, cooking takes 15 minutes.

Cook's Tip: If you want to reduce the calories in this recipe replace the cream with yogurt.

Spaghetti Dolce

This is a very simple pasta dish – a nursery pudding for big children!

SERVES 4

6 ounces spaghetti

⅔ cup heavy cream

2 Tbsps brandy

Sugar to taste

Cook the spaghetti in plenty of boiling water for 10-12 minutes or, until *al dente*. Drain and rinse in boiling water, then drain again, and place the spaghetti in a warm serving dish.

Mix together the cream and brandy, adding sugar to taste and pour this over the hot spaghetti. Toss, then serve immediately.

Time: Cooking takes about 12 minutes.

Honey & Cardamom —Macaroni—

Honey and cardamom make the most delightful aromatic flavorings for this macaroni dessert.

SERVES 4

4 ounces macaroni

2 cups full-cream milk

3-4 Tbsps clear honey, or to taste

1 tsp cardamom seeds, lightly ground

⅔ cup sour cream or crème fraîche

Grated lemon rind to decorate

Place the macaroni, milk, and honey in a large pan and cook until the macaroni is tender. Stir frequently, being careful not to allow the milk to boil over. Take the pan off the heat and stir in the ground cardamom seeds. Allow the macaroni to cool slightly, then stir in the crème fraîche or sour cream. Pour into a serving dish and top with grated lemon rind before serving.

Time: Preparation takes 5 minutes, cooking takes about 15 minutes.

Honey Vermicelli

Honey, sesame, and cinnamon give a Greek flavor to this pasta dessert.

SERVES 4

8 ounces vermicelli

5 Tbsps sour cream

5 Tbsps heavy cream

¼ cup butter

2 tsps sesame seeds

3 Tbsps clear honey

¼ tsp cinnamon

Cook the vermicelli in boiling water for 5 minutes or until tender, stirring regularly with a fork to separate the noodles. Drain, and spread out to dry on a wire tray covered with absorbent kitchen paper. Leave for about 1 hour.

Make a sauce by mixing the sour cream and heavy cream together. Melt the butter in a skillet. Add the sesame seeds and fry until lightly browned. Stir in the honey, cinnamon, and vermicelli, and heat gently. Serve hot, topped with the cream sauce.

Time: Preparation takes 1 hour, cooking takes 15 minutes.

Variation: For a healthier alternative, serve the vermicelli topped with plain yogurt instead of cream.

Penne with Raisins & Poppyseeds

This is a traditional Polish dish, served on Christmas Eve. Poppyseeds make a delicious crunchy coating over pasta.

SERVES 6

Pinch of salt

1 Tbsp oil

8 ounces penne

⅔ cup heavy cream

⅔ cup black poppyseeds, coarsely ground

2 Tbsps honey

⅔ cup dark or yellow raisins

Bring plenty of water to a boil in a large pan with a pinch of salt. Add the oil and pasta and return to a boil. Cook for about 10-12 minutes, or until *al dente*. Drain and rinse the pasta under hot water. If using immediately, allow to drain dry. If not, place in a bowl of hot water to keep moist.

Place the cream in a deep, heavy-based pan and bring almost to a boil. When the cream is almost boiling, mix in the poppyseeds, honey, and raisins. Cook slowly for about 5 minutes. The mixture should become thick but still fall off a spoon easily. Toss the poppyseed mixture with the drained pasta and serve hot.

Time: Preparation takes 15 minutes, cooking takes 15 minutes.

Peach Brulée

The combination of peaches and creamy macaroni make this a real brulée surprise.

SERVES 4

4 ounces small pasta shapes for soup

2 large, ripe peaches

1 cup heavy cream, lightly whipped

2 Tbsps sugar

Light brown sugar

Cook the pasta in plenty of boiling water for about 8 minutes, until tender. Drain, rinse in cold water and then drain again. Cut the peaches in half, pit them, and skin them. Cut the halves into slices and lay in a fan pattern in the bottom of four individual ovenproof dishes.

Mix the cooled pasta with the whipped cream, then stir in the sugar to taste. Spoon the mixture into the ovenproof dishes, over the peaches. Leave until quite cold.

Preheat the broiler until very hot. Place a thick layer of light brown sugar all over the top of the creamed macaroni, then quickly broil, until the sugar has melted and caramelized. Chill the brulées slightly before serving.

Time: Preparation takes 10 minutes, plus chilling. Cooking takes about 10 minutes.

Creamy Macaroni with Apricot Purée

A slightly sharp apricot purée makes an excellent sauce to serve with a dish of rich, sweet pasta.

SERVES 4

2 cups fresh apricots, or 1 cup dried apricots

²/₃ cup water

Grated rind and juice of 1 lemon

¹/₂ cup superfine sugar

6 ounces macaroni

1¹/₄ cups heavy cream

If the apricots are fresh, pit them. Place the fresh or dried fruit in a pan with the water and lemon rind and juice. Cover and simmer for about 10 minutes, or until soft. Press the fruit through a strainer or blend in a blender or food processor until smooth. Add 2-3 tablespoons of the sugar and a little extra water if necessary.

While the apricots are cooking, bring a large pan of water to a boil. Add the macaroni and cook for 10-12 minutes, or until *al dente*. Drain and rinse in boiling water, then drain again. Heat the cream gently with the remaining sugar, then add the macaroni and toss well. Serve the pasta with the apricot purée marbled through it.

Time: Preparation takes 10 minutes, cooking takes 20 minutes.

Vanilla Cream Melba

Sweet pasta puddings make substantial desserts to serve after a light main course or salad.

SERVES 4

⅓ cup small pasta shapes for soup

2 cups milk

3 Tbsps soft brown sugar

Few drops of vanilla extract

⅔ cup heavy cream, lightly whipped

14-ounce can peach halves

1 tsp cinnamon (optional)

Melba sauce

1 cup raspberries

2 Tbsps powdered sugar

Cook the pasta in the milk and sugar until soft. Stir frequently, being careful not to let the milk to boil over. Take off the heat and stir in the vanilla extract. Pour the pasta into a bowl to cool it. When cool, fold in the cream and chill.

Meanwhile, push the raspberries through a strainer, then mix in the powdered sugar to the required thickness and taste. Serve the pasta with the peach halves and Melba sauce. If wished, dust with a little cinnamon to decorate.

Time: Preparation takes 15 minutes, cooking takes 10 minutes.

Cook's Tip: Use fresh peaches when they are in season, as they taste much better than canned peaches.

Eight Treasure —Macaroni—

This is a variation on the classic Chinese dessert of Eight Treasure Rice. It is slightly less rich when made with macaroni.

SERVES 4

6 ounces macaroni

1¼ cups heavy cream

1 cup sweetened chestnut purée

15 dried red dates

2 Tbsps large raisins

4 Tbsps walnut halves

2 Tbsps almonds

4 Tbsps candied cherries, halved

¼ cup angelica, chopped

¼ cup papaya or mango, chopped

Cook the macaroni in plenty of boiling water for 10-12 minutes, or until just *al dente*. Drain, rinse in boiling water, then drain again. Return the macaroni to the saucepan and stir in the cream and chestnut purée. Heat gently until the chestnut purée has melted into the macaroni.

Roughly chop the dates, raisins, and nuts, then add them to the warm macaroni with the remaining ingredients. Stir carefully, then serve the dessert warm.

Time: Preparation takes 10 minutes, cooking takes about 20 minutes.

Chocolate Cream Helene

Pears and chocolate are a classic combination – with a pasta cream the pudding is a little more substantial.

SERVES 4

⅓ cup small pasta shapes for soup
2 cups milk
1½ Tbsps sugar
1 tsp cocoa
1 Tbsp hot water
⅔ cup heavy cream, lightly whipped
14-ounce can pear halves
Decoration
Chocolate, grated

Cook the pasta in the milk and sugar until soft. Stir frequently, being careful not to allow the milk to boil over.

Meanwhile, dissolve the cocoa in the hot water, then stir it into the pasta. Pour the pasta into a bowl to cool.

When cool, fold in the lightly whipped cream and chill. Serve the pasta cream with the pear halves and a sprinkling of grated chocolate.

Time: Preparation takes 15 minutes, cooking takes 10 minutes.

Variation: Use other soft fruits, such as strawberries, instead of the pears.

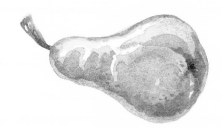

Cream Cheese Margherita

Margherita is most often thought of as a drink or a pizza! Here it's a delicious pasta dessert.

SERVES 4

½ cup yellow raisins
Grated rind and juice of ½ lemon
½ cup small pasta shapes for soup
1 cup cream cheese
2 Tbsps superfine sugar
⅔ cup light cream
½ tsp ground cinnamon
Decoration
1 Tbsp slivered almonds
Lemon rind, cut into slivers

Soak the yellow raisins in the lemon juice for about 1 hour. Meanwhile, cook the pasta in plenty of boiling water for 8 minutes, or until *al dente*, stirring occasionally. Drain and cool.

Beat the cream cheese, sugar, and cream together until smooth, then beat in the grated lemon rind and cinnamon. Fold in the pasta and yellow raisins. Divide the mixture between 4 sundae glasses, then sprinkle with the slivered almonds and the slivers of lemon peel. Chill before serving.

Time: Preparation takes 1 hour, cooking takes 10 minutes.

Variation: Substitute other chopped dried fruits, such as apricots, for the yellow raisins.

Index